D0236145

The Crafter's Year

The Crafter's Year

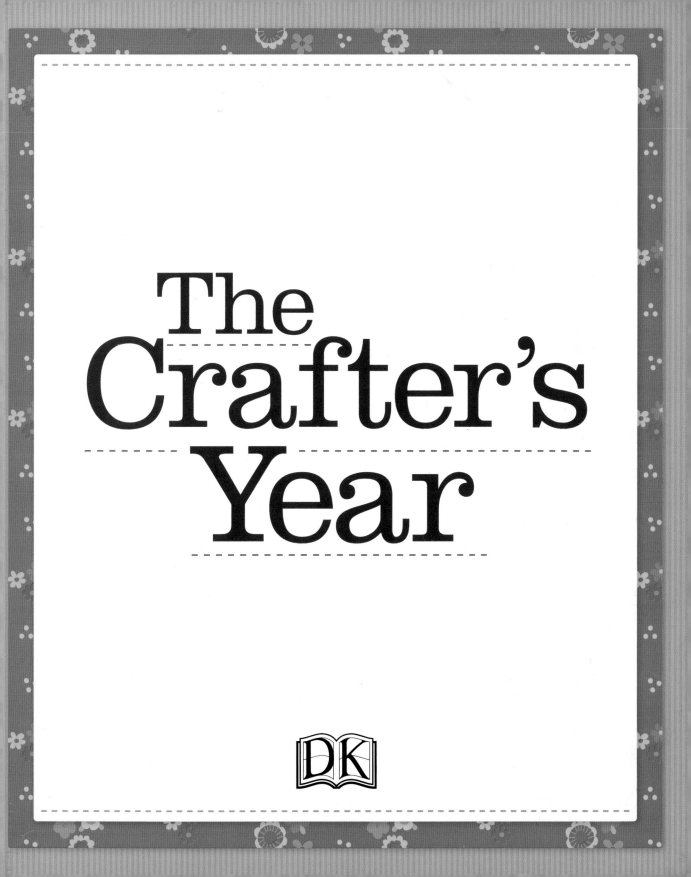

Designer and Illustrator Vanessa Hamilton
Project Editor Elizabeth Yeates
Jacket Designer Amy Keast
Pre-Production Producer Rebecca Fallowfield
Senior Producer Ché Creasy
Special Sales Creative Project Manager Alison Donovan

A Penguin Random House Company
001-290931-Feb/2016

A CIP catalogue record for this book is available from the British Library
ISBN: 978-0-2412-4831-7

Printed and bound in China

A WORLD OF IDEAS
SEE ALL THERE IS TO KNOW

www.dk.com

CONTENTS

SPRING

SUMMER

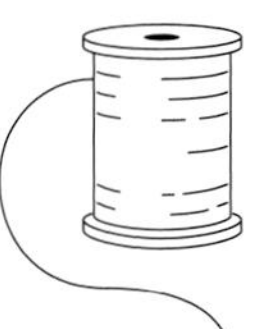

AUTUMN

WINTER

INTRODUCTION

Whether you are a beginner or a seasoned craftsperson, there is always a new craft to try and a new project to make. In *The Crafter's Year*, there is an array of inspirational projects for you to undertake, keeping you busy all the way through the four seasons.

Decorate ceramics, make bunting, and create balcony planters in spring. In summer try your hand at a child's sun bonnet, a stencilled beach bag, or some pretty mosaic flowerpots. As autumn arrives, make a teacup candle, felt brooches, and fizzy bath bombs. And with the onset of winter, make your own Christmas decorations, a hot water bottle cover, or a tartan jacket for your dog.

There are also seasonal foodie projects: make macarons in spring, raspberry jam in summer, plum chutney in autumn, and chocolate truffles in winter.

All the projects are broken down into manageable steps to help you produce perfect results. Specific techniques are carefully explained and easy to follow. Take your time, follow the instructions carefully, and you'll soon have created a piece to be proud of: something to take pride of place in your home or garden, something to wear, or something to give away as a unique present. Some of the projects also include clever variations to broaden your imagination further.

Many of the materials used in the projects you will already have in your home, and any specialist items can easily be found in a local craft shop. Lots of projects use recycled materials, too, so keep tin cans for making decorated lanterns and planters, save paper for making this year's Christmas cards, and use up scraps of yarn for making crochet jewellery.

The Crafter's Year allows you to indulge your creative side, stretch your imagination, and have lots of fun producing an amazing collection of crafts. With this book to hand, your free time will be craft time.

TOOLS AND EQUIPMENT

You may already have many of the materials used in the projects. Here are some of the more specialist pieces needed.

Fabric paints These are available in a wide range of colours that can be mixed to create your own shades.

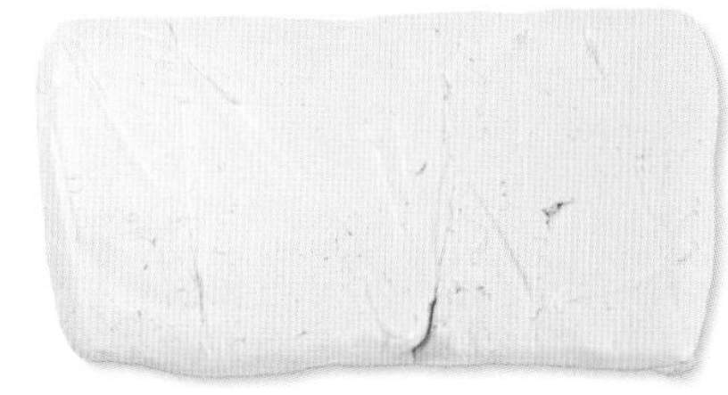

Air-dry clay As the name suggests, the appeal of air-dry clay is that it hardens in the air. Some air-dry clays shrink a little as they dry out. Keep the clay wrapped in clingfilm and in an airtight container when not in use.

Foam block You'll need a fairly deep block of foam sponge when dry needle-felting to work the fleece fibres on.

Felting needles
These long, sharp, needles compress and mould dry fleece fibres into 3D shapes by poking the fibres into each other so that they tangle together. Use a multi-needle tool to work over a large area; for smaller projects, use a single-needle tool.

Washable PVA
Polyvinyl acetate is a white liquid glue. The water-soluble variety, often sold as school glue, is used in a dilute form (50:50 with water) to stick tiles to paper.

Jump rings Use these tiny findings to join fastenings to necklaces and to link components. Do not pull the rings open outwards as they may weaken and snap.

Masonry nails
These nails are hardened so they are an ideal choice for punching through a tin can.

Ceramic paints These specialist paints come in an array of colours. Read the manufacturer's instructions to see how durable they are once baked.

Cement-based adhesive Tiling adhesives are based on traditional sand and cement but contain additives to improve adhesion. Different types are available for different applications – always read the manufacturer's label to be sure you have the right product.

Découpage medium This is the best choice of adhesive to stick down paper cutouts.

Hand carders Use carders to blend fibres and straighten out unruly tufts of fleece. They come as a pair. The edge nearest the handle is called the "heel" and the opposite edge is the "toe".

Unglazed ceramic mosaic tiles Unglazed ceramic is a hard-wearing material that can be used on walls and floors. Tiles come in two sizes, 2 x 2cm (¾ x ¾in) and 24 x 24mm (1 x 1in), and in an attractive range of muted colours.

Tile nippers This is the essential tool for mosaic cutting and can be used on all mosaic materials. The blades must be tungsten-tipped. It's worth paying a bit more to get a pair that will cut accurately.

Colourants Cosmetic pigments, dyes, and micas (powdered minerals) offer a safe and lasting way to colour soap. Food colours can also be used but are prone to fading so are best avoided.

Firing brick and mesh To protect your work surface, place metal clay pieces on a sheet of stainless steel mesh over a heatproof fibre brick while heating them with a torch.

Fabric paint pens Use these to outline edges and define shapes once the main design is complete.

Dyes These are available in flake and liquid forms. Flakes are easy to cut, measure, and handle, and produce no mess.

Scents Essential oils are ideal for creating aromatherapy soaps, while synthetic fragrances offer a range of additional scent options. Only use essential oils or fragrances that are safe for cosmetic use.

gel wax

soy wax

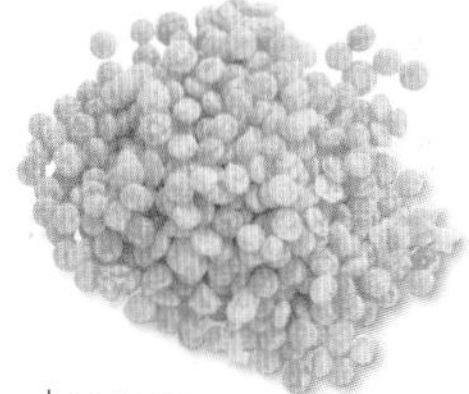

beeswax

Wax There are different types of wax: beeswax, soy wax, gel wax, and petroleum (paraffin) wax. Beeswax and soy wax are natural, clean-burning products. Soy wax is available in flakes and, as it is water-soluble, it is easy to remove from pans and utensils after use.

Cuddly cushions

Teatime planter

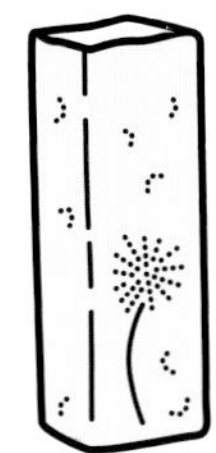

Decorated ceramics

Soft play blocks

Needle-felted flocks

Mmmm... Macarons

Finger puppets

Balcony planters

Paper flowers

SPRING

Fluttery
bunting

CUDDLY CUSHIONS

These lovable cushion covers make a charming set or can be used individually. Choose fabrics that complement each other but are different.

HOW TO MAKE A CUDDLY CUSHION

Materials

* Marker pen or pencil
* Tracing paper
* Scissors
* 40 x 40cm (16 x 16in) fusible interfacing, per cushion
* Fabrics for the animals
* Iron
* Pins
* 42 x 42cm (16½ x 16½in) square main cushion fabric & two 42 x 31cm (16½ x 12¼in) rectangles main cushion fabric, per cushion
* Contrasting thread for tacking
* Needle
* Thread to match main cushion fabric
* Sewing machine capable of zigzag stitch
* Black embroidery thread
* Light-brown thread, for giraffe's nostrils
* Large-eyed needle
* 45 x 45cm (17¾ x 17¾in) wadding, per cushion
* 45 x 45cm (17¾ x 17¾in) thin, white cotton fabric, per cushion

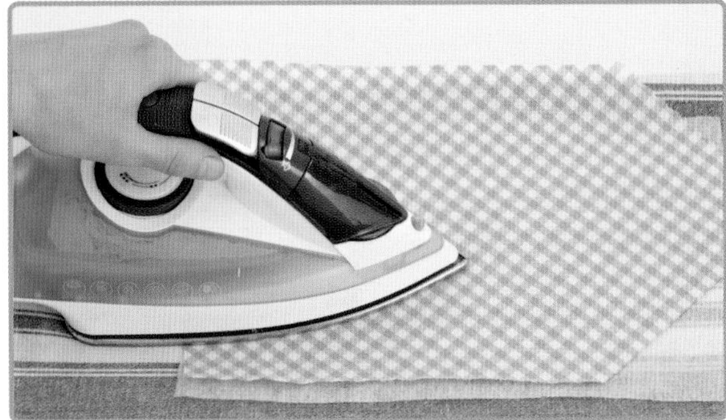

1 **With a marker pen** or pencil, trace the templates on page 17 for the lamb and giraffe onto the tracing paper. Cut out the templates.

2 **Iron the fabric** for the animal's body and the scraps for the animal details to the fusible interfacing, setting your iron to warm, not hot. Cut the fusible interfacing as required before you start. Make sure the shiny side of the interfacing is against the wrong side of the fabric. Press firmly on the iron until the fabric and interfacing have fused together.

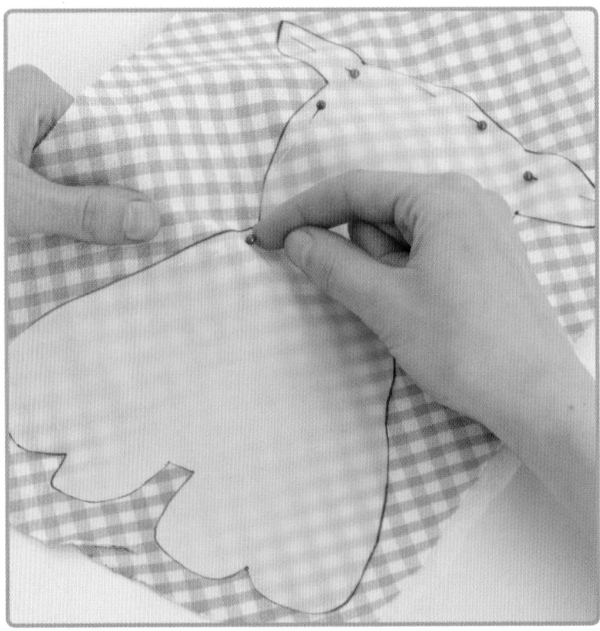

3 **Pin your template** pieces to their corresponding pieces of interfaced fabric. Cut around the templates, then remove the pins and the templates. Iron the main fabric square and the two rectangles. These will form the front and back flaps of the cushion respectively.

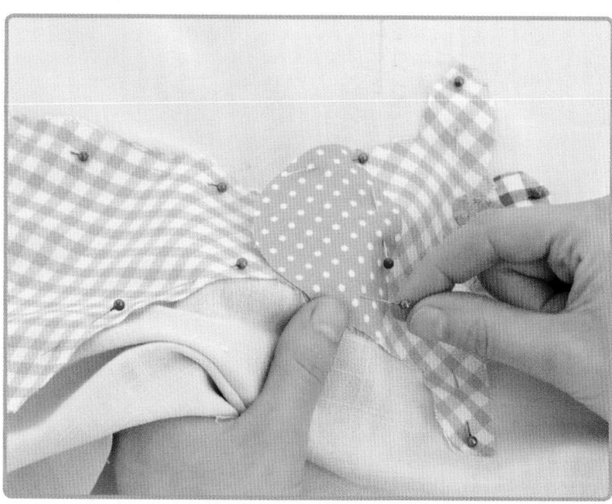

4 Centre and pin the animal's body on the front cushion fabric. If making the lamb, lay the bow and nose on top of the lamb's body. If making the giraffe, lay the hooves, nose, and forelock on top of the body and tuck the two horns slightly underneath the head. Pin all the pieces in place.

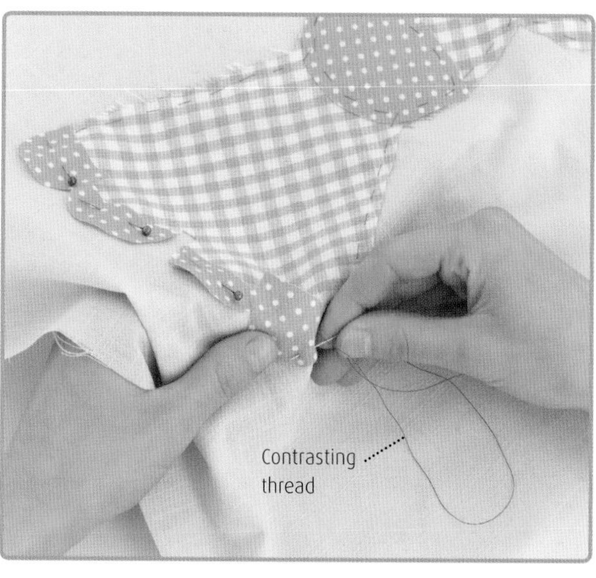

5 Using the contrasting thread, tack all the pieces in place on the front cushion fabric. Tack around the edges of every piece, however small. Remove the pins.

6 Set your sewing machine to a wide zigzag stitch with a short 0-1 stitch length, to create a close satin stitch. Thread your sewing machine and bobbin with the correct colour thread and carefully stitch along all the edges of your pieces.

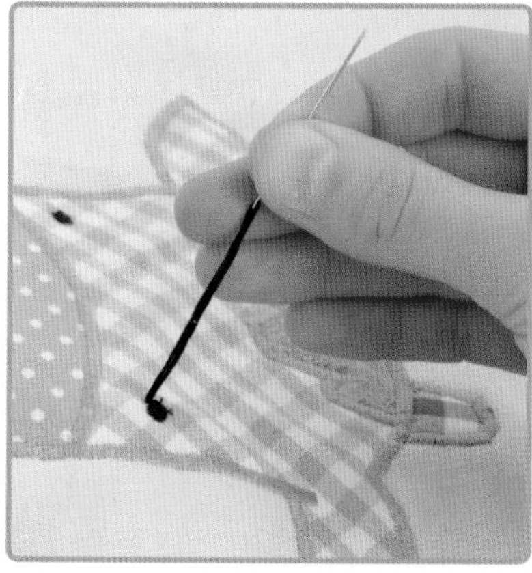

7 Once your animal is machine-stitched in place, remove all the tacking stitches. Thread the large-eyed needle with black embroidery thread and embroider the animals' eyes. The giraffe also has nostrils; use light-brown thread to embroider these.

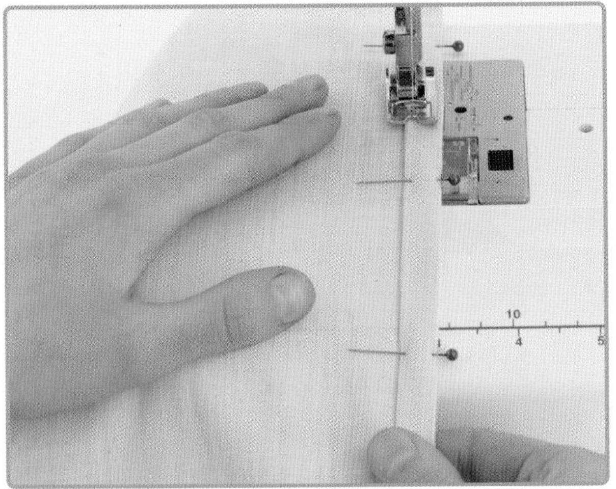

Sandwich
the wadding
between the
white cotton
and cushion
front fabric

8 **Hem one long edge** on each of the back flaps by folding it over twice, each time by 1cm (½in). Pin in place as shown. Thread your sewing machine and bobbin with matching thread and re-set the machine to a straight stitch of normal width and length. Stitch close to the edge of the fold. Remove the pins. Repeat on the second flap. Next, cut a piece of wadding and a piece of thin, white cotton, each 42 x 42cm (16½ x 16½in) square.

9 **Place the white cotton** on your work surface and top it with the wadding. Top that with the cushion front, right side up. Place one of the back flaps on top, right side down, aligning its unhemmed edge with the bottom edge of the cushion. Place the other back flap on top, right side down, aligning its unhemmed edge with the top edge of the cushion. The back flaps will overlap. Pin the layers of fabric together around all four sides of the cushion, aligning the edges.

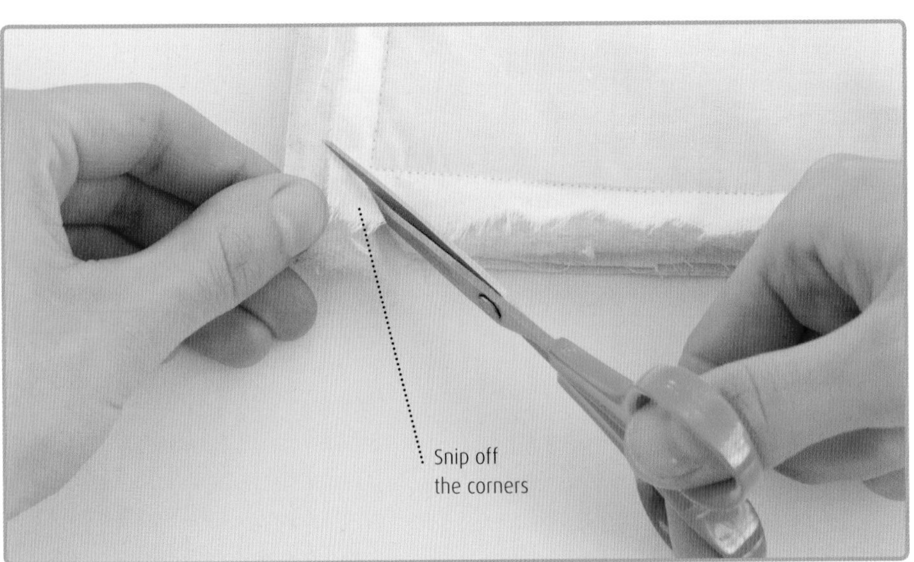

10 **Machine along** the four sides of the cushion cover using a 1cm (½in) seam allowance. Snip diagonally across the four corners to remove the excess fabric, taking care not to cut through the stitches. Turn the cushion cover right side out and iron if needed. Insert the cushion pad through the back.

TEMPLATES

Template

Enlarge by 190% on a photocopier

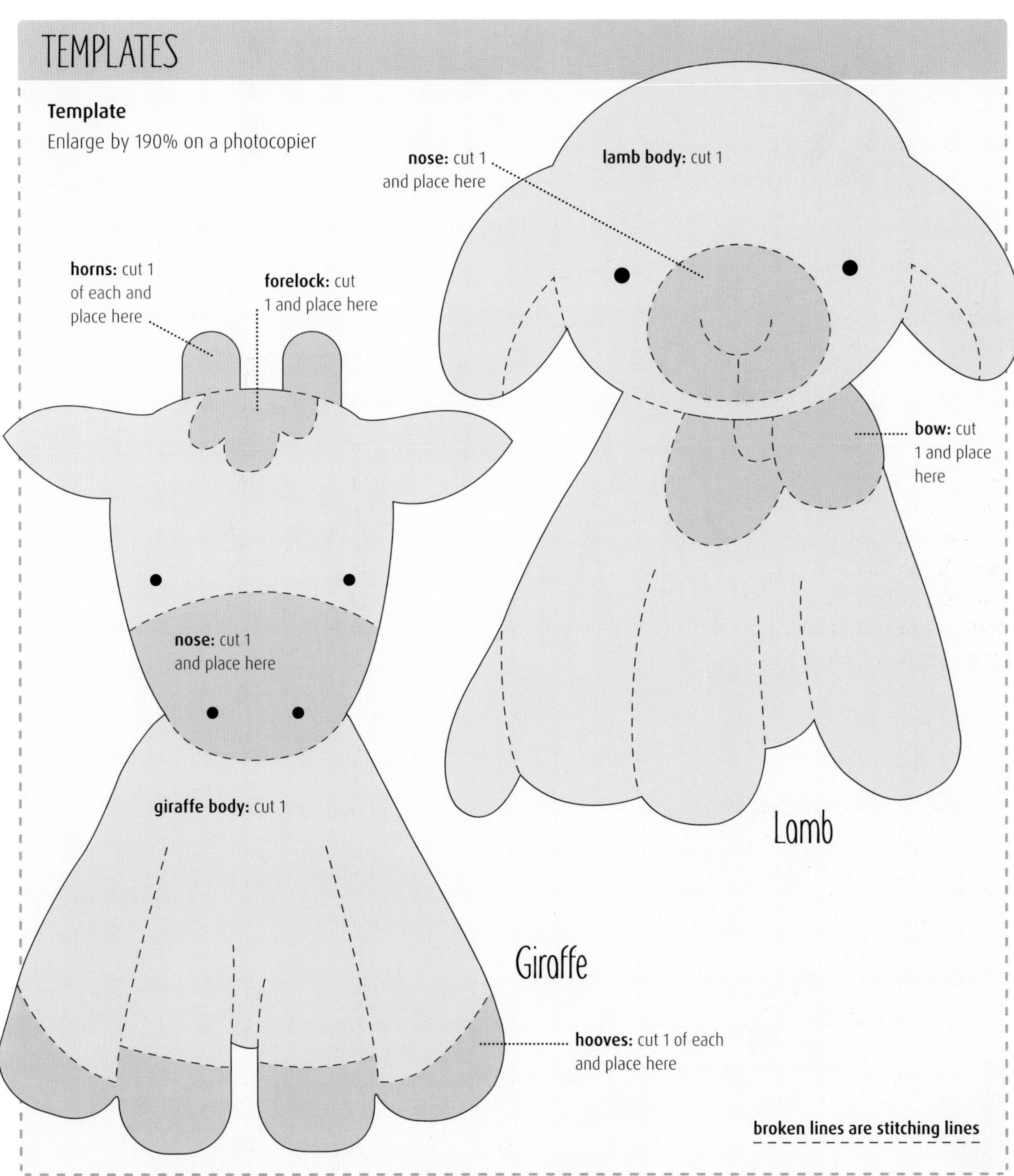

broken lines are stitching lines

TEATIME PLANTER

Enjoy traditional "afternoon tea" in the garden with this delicate tray and vintage tea set filled with dainty alpine plants.

HOW TO MAKE A TEATIME PLANTER

Materials

* Old metal tray
* Butyl liner & scissors
* Strong outdoor adhesive & paintbrush
* Vintage teacups, teapot & milk jug
* Masking tape
* Electric drill & ceramic drill bit
* Gravel & small scoop or spoon
* John Innes No.2 potting compost
* Horticultural grit
* Slow-release fertilizer granules
* Strong galvanized chain
* Wire cutters
* 3 small galvanized metal hooks
* Large galvanized metal ring
* Strong metal hanging bracket, fixed securely to a wall
* Vintage cutlery (optional)
* Silver florist wire or similar

Plant list

* Carpet moss
* *Armeria juniperifolia* 'Bevan's Variety'
* *Erigeron karvinskianus*
* *Protia peduncularis*
* *Rhodohypoxis deflexa*
* *Sisyrinchium californicum* 'Brachypus'

1 **Cut a piece** of butyl (you could use pond liner or a heavy-duty dustbin bag) to fit inside the base of the tray. Glue it into place with outdoor adhesive.

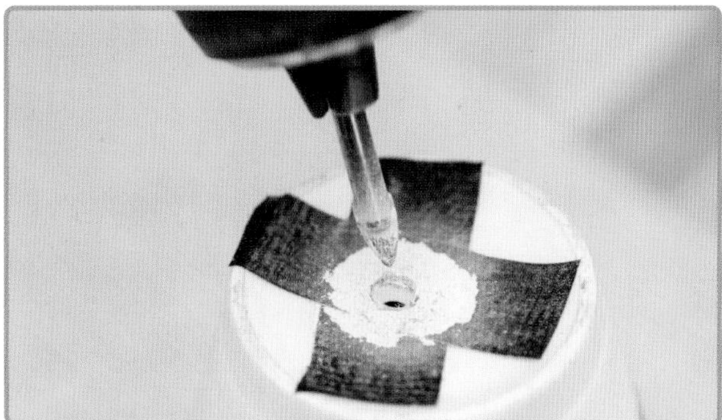

2 **Take your cups**, teapot, and milk jug and make a cross with two pieces of masking tape over the centre area where you intend to drill a hole; this helps prevent the drill from slipping and creates a clean cut. Drill drainage holes in the base of the items using an electric drill with a ceramic tile drill bit.

3 **Create an attractive** arrangement with your crockery on the lined tray and then glue the saucers in place and remove the cups, teapot, and jug for planting up.

4 **Alpines need good** drainage, so to plant up first fill the base of the crockery with a layer of gravel. Next, make a soil mix suitable for alpine plants by blending John Innes No. 2 potting compost with horticultural grit at a ratio of 3:1. At the same time, mix in a small amount of slow-release fertilizer.

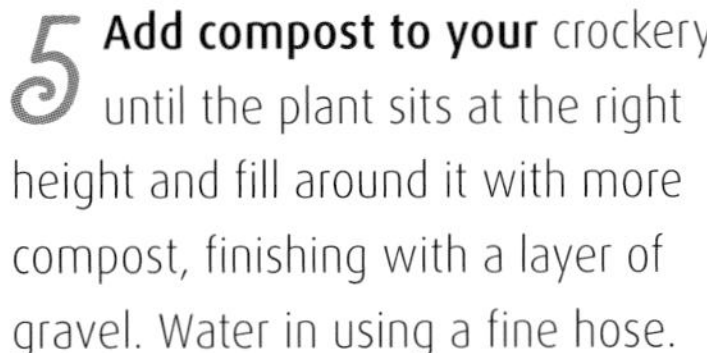

5 **Add compost to your** crockery until the plant sits at the right height and fill around it with more compost, finishing with a layer of gravel. Water in using a fine hose.

6 **Place the planted** cups on saucers and the other items on the tray and glue in place; just dab glue on one or two spots on the bottom of the cups to leave space for water to drain into the saucers. Fill around the crockery with moss.

7 **To hang, cut** three lengths of chain to the desired hanging height using wire cutters. Attach to hooks and then to the edge of the tray. Gather the chains and fix the free ends to a ring. Hang from a strong bracket. If you like, decorate the chains by attaching vintage pieces of cutlery with fine silver wire.

CARE ADVICE

WHERE TO SITE

Alpines prefer a sunny site that is not too shady and, ideally for this arrangement, one that has shelter from strong winds. During winter and freezing weather, bring your teatime planter indoors, but keep it in a cool, light place.

WATERING AND FEEDING

Alpines thrive in dry conditions in the natural world so don't overwater – just when needed from mid-spring to early autumn, with occasional watering at other times. Do not let plants sit in water for long periods of time as this could lead to rot. Alpines do not need a lot of feed so it is best to give a weak diluted liquid feed during the growing season. Do not feed when the plants are dormant.

GENERAL CARE

Trim or prune plants with small scissors or secateurs to remove spent flower stalks and dead material. Plants will eventually outgrow their teacups so plant up into larger containers or borders elsewhere in the garden.

OTHER IDEAS

All-year colour

Evergreen alpines, such as sempervivums (above) and sedums, are ideal for planting in small containers, and will provide year-round interest. Although many form flowers, most are grown for their foliage, which can be very colourful.

Seasonal flowers

Flowering alpines are ideal for injecting a splash of colour into your display, and some will bloom for several weeks. Once their flowers fade, consider replanting the container with plants that flower later for a prolonged show.

Easy living

The advantage of choosing alpine plants, such as thrift (above), is that many are drought tolerant and don't require regular feeding. This makes them very easy to look after and forgiving of neglect, which is ideal for busy households.

Mixed planters

Larger items of crockery, such as bowls and dishes, are perfect for planting small groups of plants together. Choose low, slow-growing plants, and allow them to form a colourful and harmonious colony.

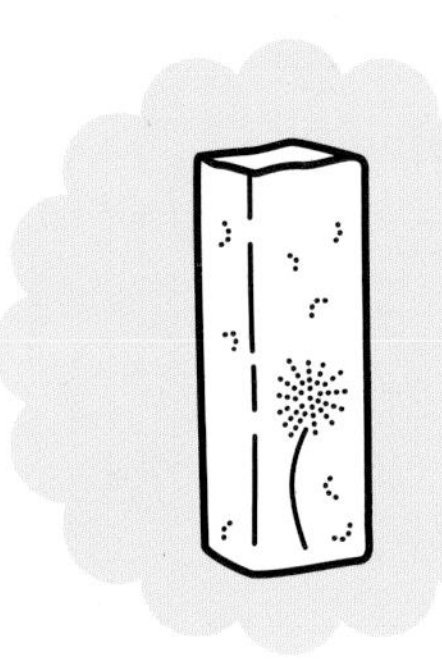

DECORATED CERAMICS

Almost any line-drawing can be turned into a dot painting, so once you have mastered the technique try out your own designs.

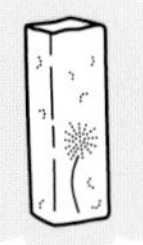

HOW TO DECORATE CERAMICS

Materials

* Ceramic vase
* Ballpoint pen
* Tracing paper
* Scissors
* Baby wipes or damp cloth
* Red transfer paper
* Masking tape
* Black, food-safe ceramic pen or paint in a dispenser

1 **Clean the vase** to remove any loose dust or grease from the surface. Draw a design of your choice onto tracing paper (with a mix of dots and solid lines) and cut it to fit the vase.

2 **Place a sheet** of transfer paper behind the template and cut out each motif. Tape to the vase, with the transfer paper underneath.

3 **Using a ballpoint pen**, firmly trace the design onto the vase. Use solid lines across some of the dots as these show up best.

4 **Remove the template** and check that the lines are visible. If not, wipe away the trace lines and repeat the process, pressing down more firmly.

5 **Use a ceramic** paint pen or paint to draw the solid lines in one continuous motion.

6 **Using the template** as a guide, complete the design with dots. Keep the spacing of the dots even and work quickly to avoid the paint pooling. Let the paint dry and repeat Steps 3–5 on each side of the vase.

7 **When the paint** is completely dry, use a baby wipe or damp cloth to wipe off the trace lines. Follow the paint manufacturer's instructions to set the paint.

ALSO TRY...

Use the dot-decorating method to create a stunning display plate; this bunting plate is the perfect gift for a celebration. Add a personal message to make the gift even more unique.

When painting dots, remember to work left to right (right to left if left-handed) to avoid smudging any paint. Why not create a set of mugs in the same design using different colours – one for each family member.

SOFT PLAY BLOCKS

These easy-to-make patchwork blocks are filled with a soft stuffing. Once you've made one block, you're sure to want to make more – which gives baby even more fun!

HOW TO MAKE SOFT PLAY BLOCKS

Materials

* Pencil or marker pen
* Tracing paper
* Scissors
* Tailor's chalk or water-soluble pen
* One 13cm (5in) Charm Pack™, containing a minimum of 36 fabrics, in the fabrics of your choice (12 charm squares are needed to make one block)
* Small scraps of different-coloured fabric for motif features
* Pins
* Sewing needle
* Tacking thread
* Threads to match your fabrics
* Seam ripper (optional)
* Dark embroidery thread
* Large-eyed needle
* Ruler or quilter's ruler
* Sewing machine
* Toy filling

1 **Using a pencil** or marker pen, draw designs of your choice onto tracing paper and cut them out. With the tailor's chalk or a water-soluble pen, trace each design onto the fabric scraps. (We have used a pencil so that readers can see the lines easily.)

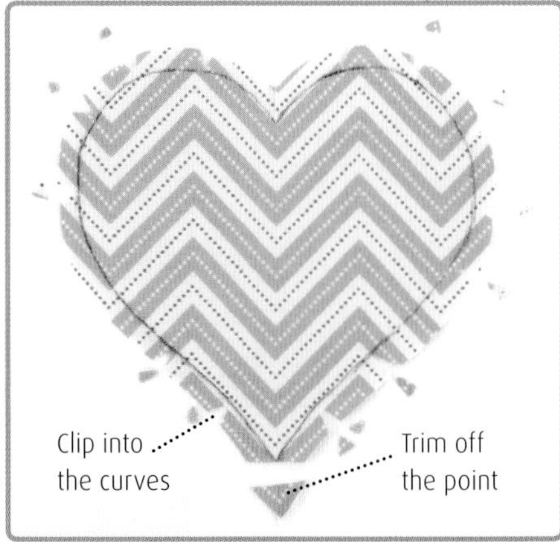
Clip into the curves
Trim off the point

2 **Cut out** the shapes, leaving a 6mm (¼in) seam allowance around each one. Clip any curves and trim off any points. You will need one set of each of the six shapes for each block you're making.

3 **Centre the pattern piece** on a contrasting square of fabric and pin it in place.

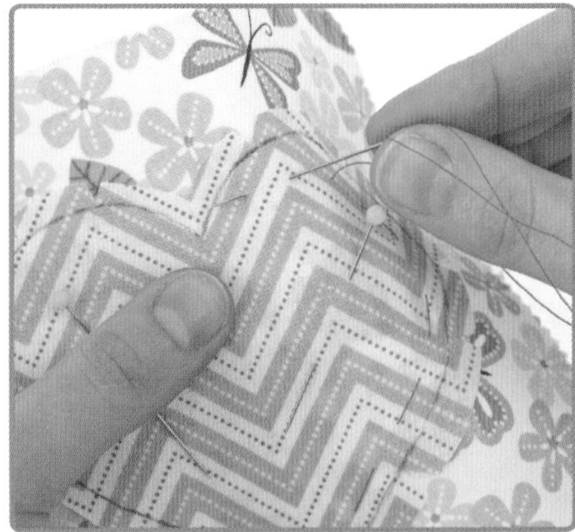

4 **Tack the pattern piece** in place around the edge, about 1cm (½in) inside the marked line.

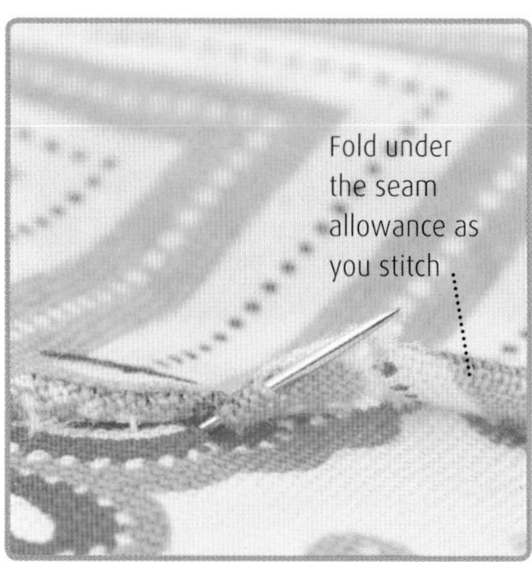
Fold under
the seam
allowance as
you stitch

Remove the tacks

Mark a dot
inside the
corner

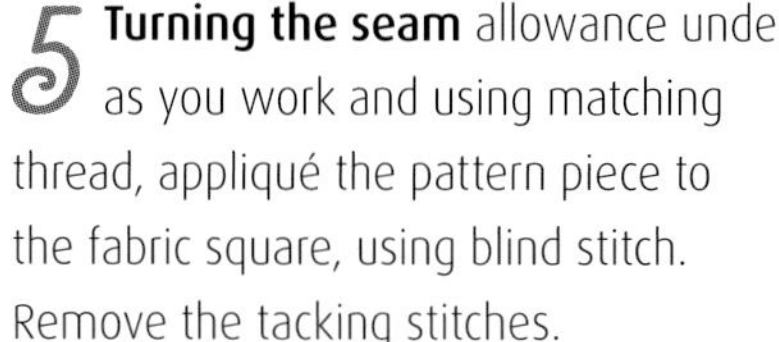

5 **Turning the seam** allowance under as you work and using matching thread, appliqué the pattern piece to the fabric square, using blind stitch. Remove the tacking stitches.

6 **Repeat Steps 3–5** to appliqué each shape to a contrasting fabric square and to attach extra motifs. Use embroidery thread and a large-eyed needle, to embroider any facial features.

7 **To prepare to sew** set-in seams, mark a dot 6mm (¼in) inside each corner on the back of each fabric square.

Only stitch to the dot

8 **Pin two squares**, right sides together, along one edge. Sew the squares together between the two marked dots, taking care not to sew beyond the dots.

9 **Continue to sew** the squares together, stitching between the dots, until they form the shape of a cross, as above. Six squares form one block. Following the arrows above, join together to form the block.

10 **Leave the final seam** unstitched for turning through. Turn the block to the right side and stuff firmly with toy filling. Slip stitch the final seam closed.

NEEDLE-FELTED FLOCKS

A sheep made from sheep's fleece is a perfect Easter gift or decoration. Needle felting is a very delicate craft, so time and patience are a must.

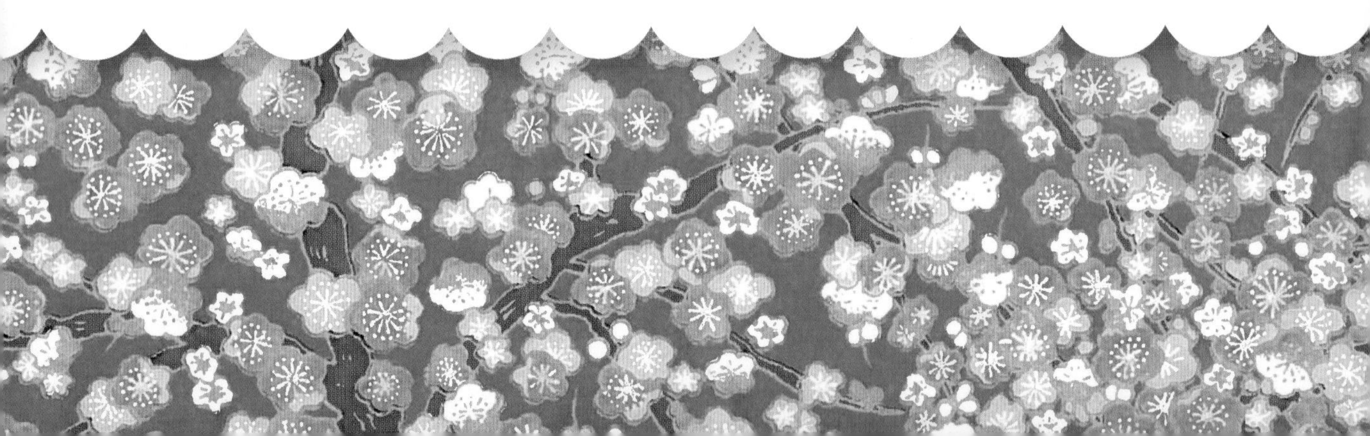

HOW TO MAKE A NEEDLE-FELTED SHEEP

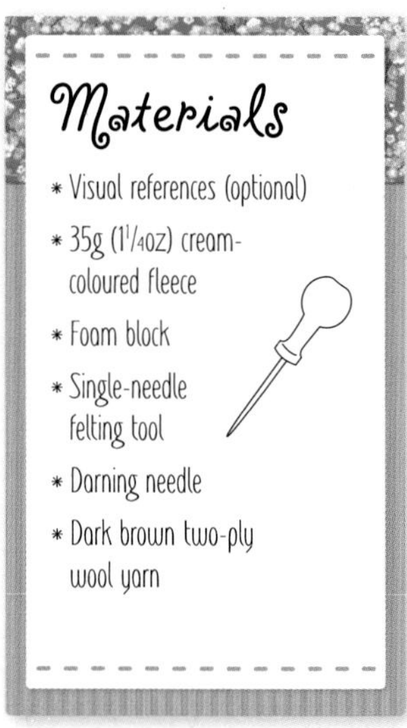

Materials

* Visual references (optional)
* 35g (1¼oz) cream-coloured fleece
* Foam block
* Single-needle felting tool
* Darning needle
* Dark brown two-ply wool yarn

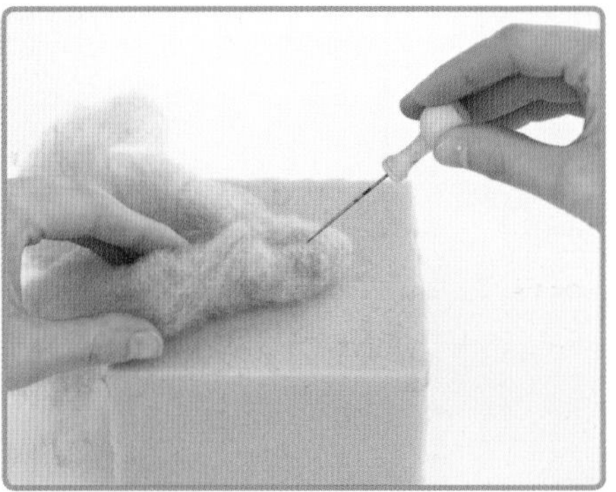

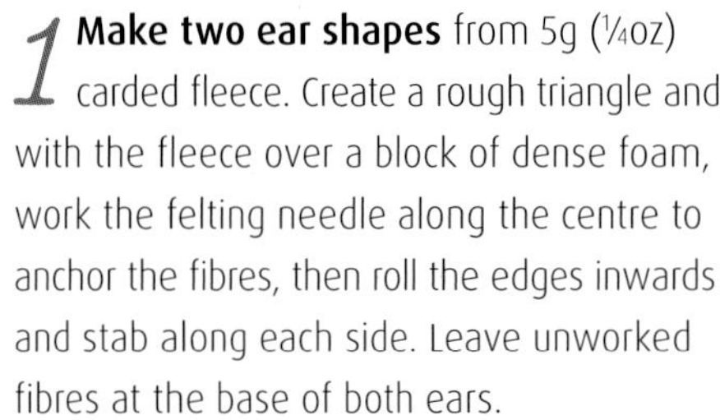

1 **Make two ear shapes** from 5g (¼oz) carded fleece. Create a rough triangle and, with the fleece over a block of dense foam, work the felting needle along the centre to anchor the fibres, then roll the edges inwards and stab along each side. Leave unworked fibres at the base of both ears.

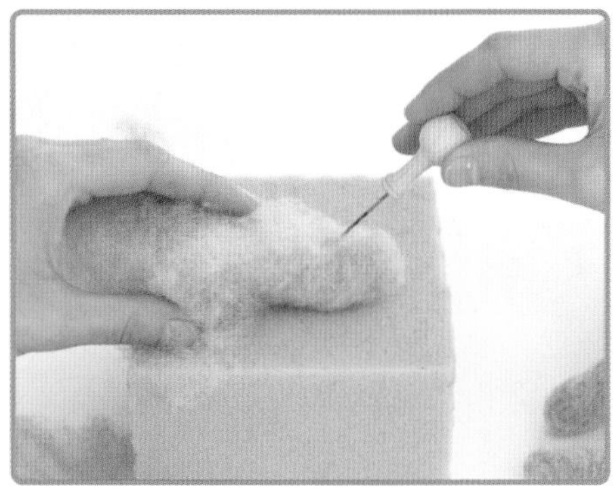

2 **Make four legs** from 12g (⅓oz) carded fleece. Roll each piece of fleece into a rough tube shape, then stab the fibres all round, turning the legs as you work. Leave unworked fibres at the top of each leg.

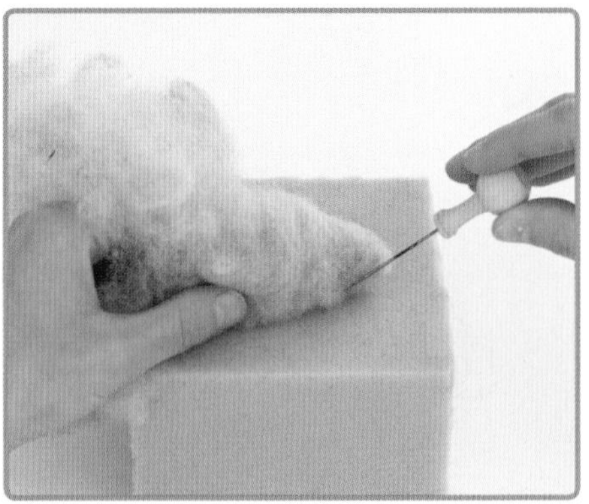

3 **Now make a head** with 5g (¼oz) carded fleece, leaving unworked fibres to attach the head to the body. Shape the nose and under the chin carefully.

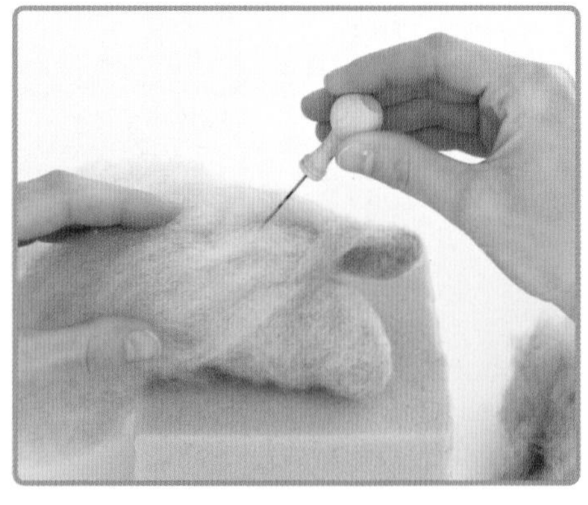

4 **Attach the ears** to the head by pinching them down the middle lengthways and laying the unworked fibres on either side of the head. Stab the felting needle through these fibres.

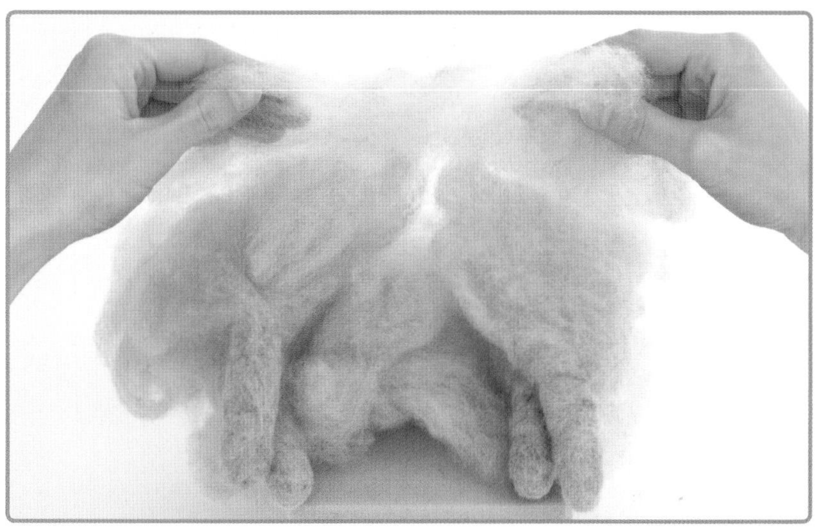

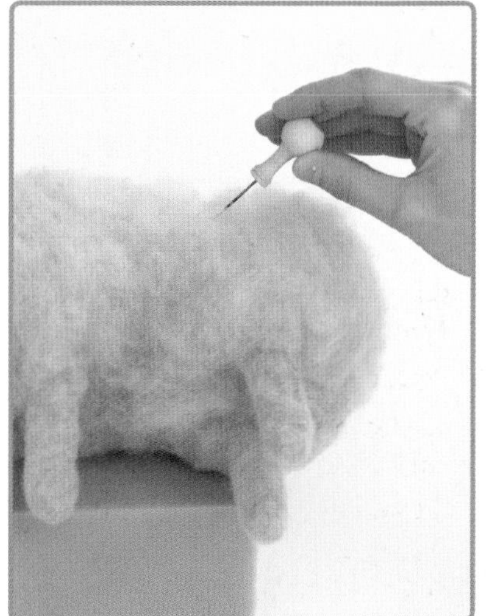

5 For the body, divide 12g (⅓oz) fleece into three and card each bundle. Lay out one bundle then place the unworked fibres of one front leg and one back leg on top of it, leaving the shaped ends protruding below the body. Place the next bundle on top, then the remaining front and back legs on top. Finally, place the last bundle over the top, to make five layers ready to be worked as a whole.

6 Lightly stab the fibres over the whole body and through all five layers, slowly compressing them to incorporate the legs and part-felt the body.

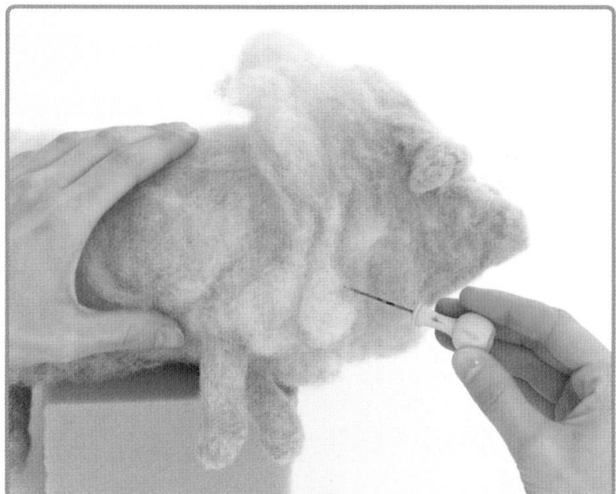

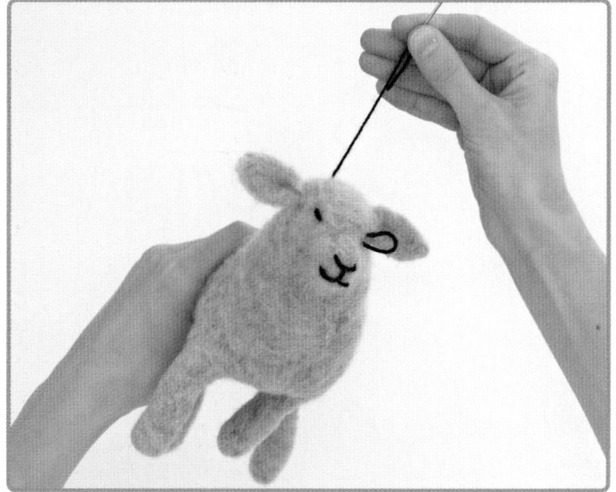

7 To attach the head, push the part-felted body into the splayed-out unworked fibres of the head, and stab the fibres so that they hold together. Continue to stab the fibres, gradually compressing them to create the body of the sheep.

8 Stitch features onto the sheep's face using one long piece of dark brown wool yarn. Start by threading it up through the chin. To finish, take the yarn back into the body and snip off close to the body to hide the end.

MMMM....
MACARONS

Light and delicate macarons make a truly sophisticated gift.
These macarons use fresh cream, so keep them chilled.

HOW TO MAKE MACARONS

Makes 20 macarons

Ingredients

- 2 large egg whites at room temperature
- 75g (2½oz) granulated sugar
- 50g (1¾oz) ground almonds
- 100g (3½oz) icing sugar
- Food colouring
- 200ml (7fl oz) double cream

Equipment

- 2 baking sheets
- Greaseproof paper
- 2 large mixing bowls
- Hand-held electric whisk
- Piping bag
- Wire cooling rack
- Hand whisk
- Palette knife

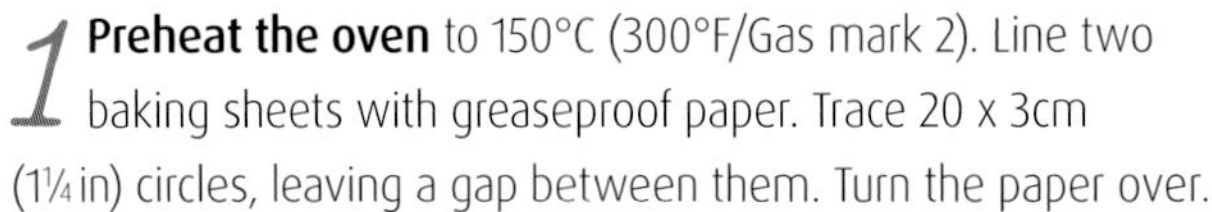

1 **Preheat the oven** to 150°C (300°F/Gas mark 2). Line two baking sheets with greaseproof paper. Trace 20 x 3cm (1¼in) circles, leaving a gap between them. Turn the paper over.

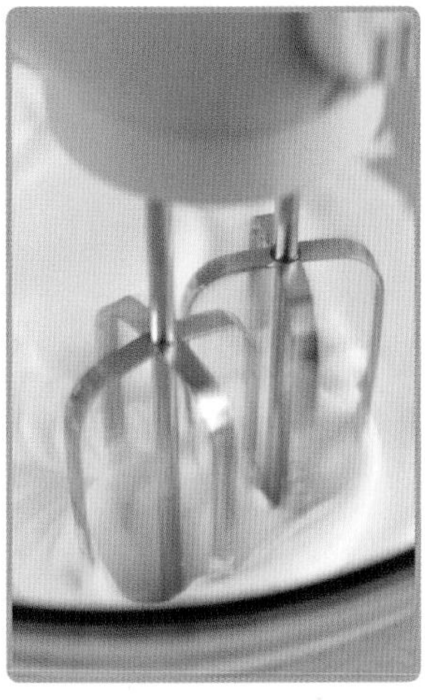

2 **In a large bowl**, whisk the egg whites to stiff peaks using an electric whisk.

3 **Add the granulated sugar** a little at a time, whisking well between additions. The meringue mixture should be very stiff at this point.

4 **Mix together** the ground almonds and the icing sugar. Gently fold in the almond mixture, a spoonful at a time, until just incorporated into the meringue mixture.

5 **Add a few drops** of pink food colouring to the mixture, folding the mixture carefully, until just mixed in.

6 **Transfer the macaron mixture** to a piping bag. Using the guidelines, pipe the mixture into the centre of each circle, allowing it to spread and fill out into an even, round shape.

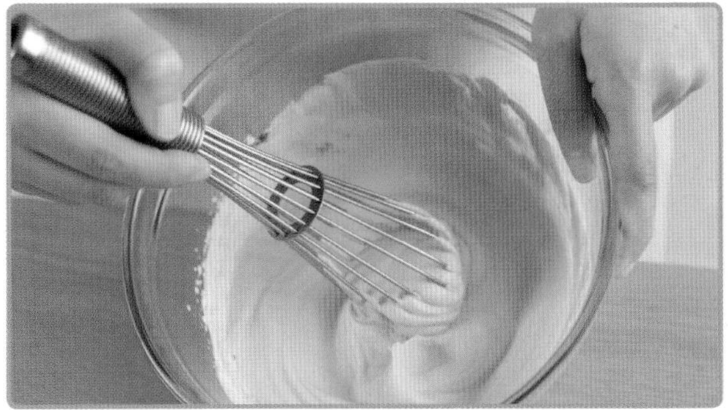

7 **Bake in the middle** of the oven for 18–20 minutes, until the surface is set firm. Leave for 15–20 minutes, then transfer to a wire rack to cool completely.

8 **Pour the double cream** into a bowl, and add some more pink food colouring. Whisk the cream until it is thick and the colour is evenly distributed.

9 **Using a palette knife**, add a blob of whipped cream to the centre of one macaron half. Add the second half and sandwich gently. Serve immediately.

FINGER PUPPETS

Give your child hours of fun making up stories of animals living in the wild. These little puppets are suited to a reasonably experienced crocheter.

FINGER PUPPETS

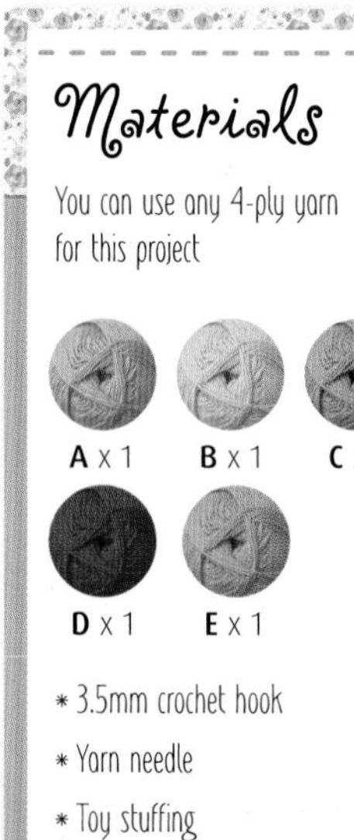

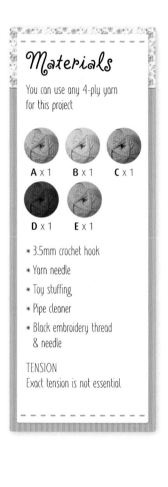

NOTE The "basic" pattern relates to all puppets. Refer to individual patterns for specific details.

Basic body

Make an adjustable ring and work 6 dc into the ring. (6sts)

Round 1 *1 dc, 2 dc in next st; repeat from * to end. (9sts)

Round 2 *2 dc, 2 dc in next st; repeat from * to end. (12sts)

Rounds 3–10 Dc in each st to end. (12sts)

Cut the yarn and pull through loop to secure. Sew in loose end and cut off.

Basic head

Make an adjustable ring and work 6 dc into the ring. (6sts)

Round 1 2 dc into each st to end. (12sts)

Round 2 *dc, 2 dc in next st; repeat from * to end. (18sts)

Round 3 *2 dc, 2 dc in next st; repeat from * to end. (24sts)

Rounds 4–6 Dc in each st to end. (24sts)

Round 7 *dc2tog, 2 dc; repeat from * to end. (18sts)

Round 8 *dc2tog, dc; repeat from * to end. (12sts)

Round 9 *dc2tog; repeat from * to end. (6sts)

Cut yarn, leaving a long tail, and pull through to secure. Stuff firmly.

Weave the yarn through the last 6 sts, pull to close at the base of head. Sew onto body and weave in loose end.

Basic arm

Make an adjustable ring and work 4 dc into the ring. (4sts)

Rounds 1–3 Dc in each st to the end. (4sts)

Cut and secure the yarn leaving a long tail. Stuff the arms, then weave the yarn end through the last 4 sts. Pull to close at top of arm. Sew in place and weave in loose ends.

ELEPHANT

Make one Basic body, one Basic head, and two Basic arms in yarn C.

Ears (make 2)

This is not worked in a spiral. Turn your work at the end of each row to form a semi circle.

With yarn C, make an adjustable ring and work 4 dc into the ring. (4sts)

Row 1 *dc, 2 dc in next st; repeat from * to end, ch 1, turn. (6sts)

Row 2 2 dc, 2 dc in next st, 1 dc, 1 htr, 2 htr in last st. (8sts)

Cut yarn, leaving a long tail, and secure. Sew in place and weave in loose ends.

Trunk

With yarn C, make an adjustable ring and work 4 dc into the ring. (4sts)

Rounds 1–8 Dc in each st to the end. (4sts)

Cut yarn, leaving a long tail, and secure. Cut a pipe cleaner to the length of the trunk and place inside. Weave yarn end through last 4 sts. Pull to close at base of trunk. Sew in place and weave in loose ends.

Tail

With yarn C, ch 8, ss in second ch from hook, ss along ch. (7sts)
Cut yarn and secure. Sew in place and weave in loose ends.

Finishing

With black embroidery thread, add the facial details. Make two French knots for the eyes.

LION

Make one Basic body, one Basic head, and two Basic arms in yarn A.

Mane

See loop stitch box (right). With yarn B, ch 26, ss to join and form a loop. (26sts)
Rounds 1–2 Loop stitch in each stitch. (26sts)
Cut yarn, leaving long tail, and secure. Sew in place on head. Weave in loose ends.

Tail

With yarn A, ch 12, ss in second ch from hook, ss along ch. (11sts)
Cut yarn and secure. Sew in place and weave in loose ends. Cut two strands of yarn B, fold in half and sew to end of tail to form tassel.

Finishing

With black embroidery thread, add the facial details. Make two French knots for the eyes, a small triangle for the nose, and lines to form the mouth. Weave in loose ends.

MONKEY

Make one Basic body, one Basic head, and two Basic arms in yarn D.

Muzzle

With yarn E, make an adjustable ring and work 6 dc into the ring. (6sts)
Round 1 Dc in each st to the end. (6sts)
Cut yarn, leaving a long tail, and secure. Weave yarn through last 6 sts and pull to close at base of body. Sew onto head and weave in loose ends.

Ears (make 2)

With yarn D, make an adjustable ring and work 8 dc into the ring, ss to join ring. (8sts)
Cut yarn and pull through to secure. Sew in place and weave in loose ends.

Eye patches

With yarn E, make an adjustable ring and work 8 dc into the ring, ss to join ring. (8sts)
Cut yarn and pull through to secure. Sew in place and weave in loose ends.

Tail

With yarn D, ch 12, ss in second ch from hook, ss along ch. (11sts.)
Cut yarn and secure. Sew in place and weave in yarn and cut off any loose ends.

Finishing

With black embroidery thread, add the facial details. Make two French knots in the centre of the eye patches for the eyes.

LOOP STITCH

Wrap the yarn from front to back over the index finger of your yarn hand. Insert the hook in the next stitch, grab the strand of yarn from behind your index finger and draw the yarn through the stitch. The yarn on your finger becomes the loop. With the yarn loop still on your index finger, yarn over the hook and draw the yarn through the two loops on your hook.

BALCONY PLANTERS

Just got a balcony as your garden space? These no-sew, easy-to-make saddle bag planters will give you lots of planting space for flowers, herbs, and edibles.

HOW TO MAKE BALCONY PLANTERS

Materials

* Oilcloth, single-sided
* Tape measure
* Metal rivet kit for fabrics, with post long enough to penetrate several layers of the oilcloth
* Hammer
* Plastic-coated motifs in attractive designs (we cut motifs from a woven carrier bag)
* Scissors
* Waterproof PVA glue or superglue, jar & paintbrush (optional)
* Hanging-basket liner, cut from a roll
* Water-retaining gel
* Multi-purpose compost
* Watering can

Plant list

* English lavender
* French lavender 'Papillon'
* *Nemesia denticulata* 'Confetti'
* *Pelargonium* 'Attar of Roses'
* *Pelargonium graveolens* 'Minor'
* Rosemary
* Sage 'Tricolor'
* Strawberry 'Elan'
* *Viola* 'Blue Beacon'

1 **Use a piece of oilcloth** measuring 100 x 120cm (3ft 3¼in x 3ft 11in) and fold in half neatly along the shorter edge with the pattern on the outside. Fold in one of the short ends by 2cm (¾in) and repeat twice more to create a seam.

2 **Rivet the seam in place**, starting 10cm (4in) in from the edge. To make a rivet hole in the cloth, place the plastic disc underneath and hammer the recessed end of the hole punch through the cloth.

3 **Push the rivet post** through the hole from underneath and tap the cap in place with the hammer. Add three more evenly spaced rivets to the seam, finishing 10cm (4in) in from the other side. Repeat steps 1–3 at the opposite short end.

4 **Fold in the riveted ends**, leaving enough material in the middle to allow for the width of your balustrade, so the bags can hang comfortably with the tops of the pockets just below the balustrade.

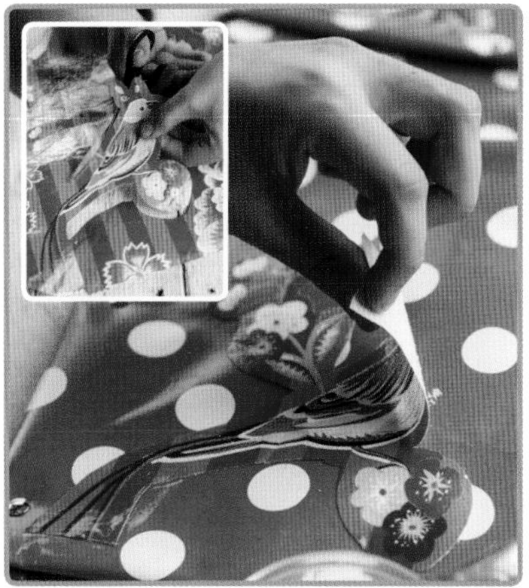

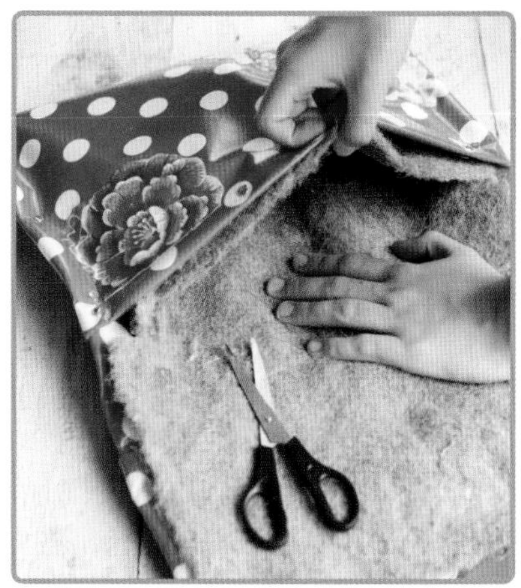

5 **Flip the cloth over**. Fold in a long side twice, including the pocket flaps, to make a 3cm (1¼in) seam. Weight the seam down to hold it as you rivet it in place. Repeat with the other long side. Flip the cloth back over and you have made your saddle bag planters. Repeat to make as many as you need.

6 **For extra ornamentation**, you can cut out some motifs from attractive reusable shopping bags to add to the saddle bags. Glue the designs on to the saddle bags with a waterproof PVA glue or superglue and then leave to dry.

7 **Take a length** of hanging-basket liner and line each of the planting pockets, cutting the liner to size with scissors. It should sit just below the lip of the pocket. This will help keep the compost moist in the pockets. To conserve moisture further, add 5g (¼oz) of water-retaining gel to every 5 litres (1 gallon) of multi-purpose compost.

8 **Hang the bags** in their final positions. Remove plants from their pots, tease out any circling roots, then position them in the pockets. Fill around with compost, and firm in. Water thoroughly.

CARE ADVICE

WATERING

Containers above ground level are more exposed and plants tend to dry out more easily, so water often in the growing season, especially if hot and sunny, and while plants are establishing.

FEEDING

Add diluted liquid feed to the water once or twice a month in the main growing season. You can also mist plants in hot weather, but not when in direct hot sunlight as the leaves might scorch.

GENERAL CARE

Remove any damaged, diseased, or dying foliage throughout the growing period. Some plants are not frost hardy and will die back if left outside in winter. Reduce watering in winter to minimal. Top up or change the compost in spring.

PAPER FLOWERS

You can make amazing paper anemones in a variety of shades. Their delicate crepe paper petals are almost impossible to distinguish from the real thing.

HOW TO MAKE PAPER FLOWERS

Materials

* Crepe paper
* Scissors
* Glue
* 20-gouge florist wire

1 **Cut two squares** of black crepe paper, then cut one in half. Stretch out the square, then scrunch one of the rectangles into a ball and wrap the other rectangle around it.

2 **Place the ball** of crepe paper in the middle of the stretched square and dot small amounts of glue around it. Holding the centre down with straight floral wire, pull the corners of the square up around the scrunched paper and wire.

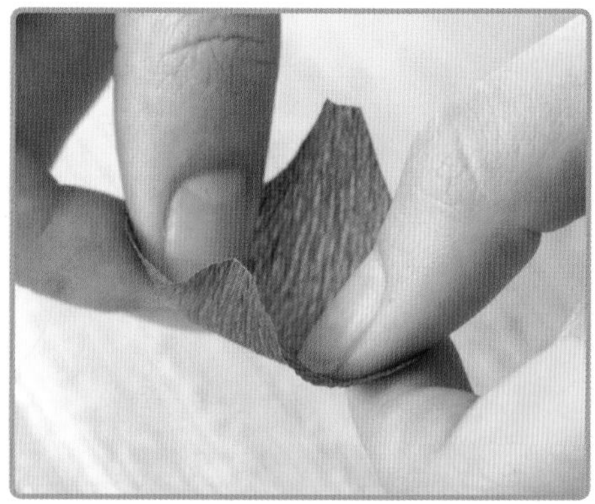

3 **Cut a strip of** purple crepe paper about 5cm (2in) long and fringe two-thirds of it. Wrap it around the black centre and glue in place, then secure with wire and paint the tips black.

4 **Using the template**, cut six petal shapes from the purple crepe paper. Push your thumbs into the centre and gently stretch outwards to give them a rounded shape.

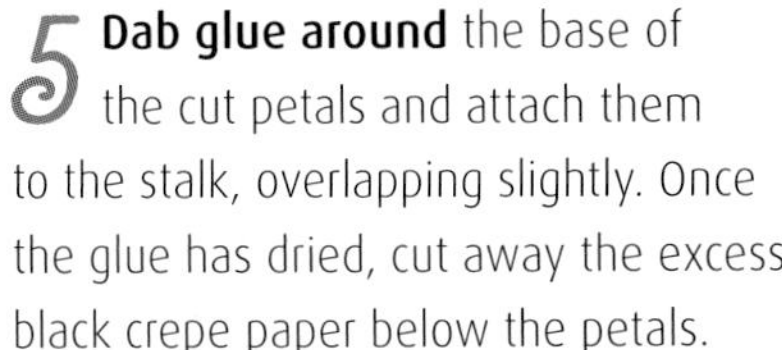

5 Dab glue around the base of the cut petals and attach them to the stalk, overlapping slightly. Once the glue has dried, cut away the excess black crepe paper below the petals.

6 Wrap the base of the flower with a long strip of green crepe paper and then wrap it down the stem diagonally. Glue in place at the bottom. Repeat until the stem is thick enough.

7 Use the template to cut four leaves from green crepe paper. Curl the leaves with scissors to give them a realistic shape, then glue them to the stem underneath the flower.

8 Finally, gently curl the tips of the petals over the scissors so that they curve inwards.

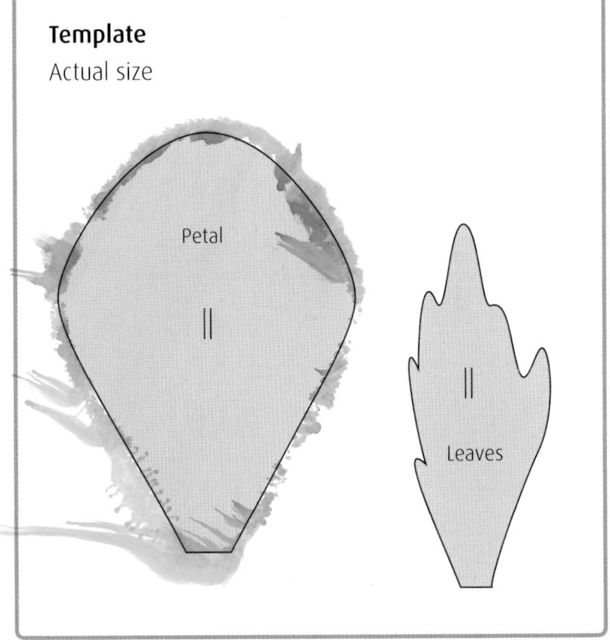

FLUTTERY BUNTING

Bunting is a quick, fun way to brighten up a party or celebration. Just remember to hang the bunting out of reach of babies and children.

HOW TO MAKE FLUTTERY BUNTING

Materials

* Tracing paper
* Pencil
* Scissors
* Selection of coordinating 17 x 22cm (6¾ x 8½in) fabrics, enough for 26 flags
* Pins
* Sewing machine
* White thread
* Pinking shears
* 3.1m (10ft 2in) of 2.5cm (1in) bias binding in the colour of your choice
* Thread to match the bias binding

1 **Draw a flag triangle** onto the tracing paper and cut it out.

2 **Pin the template** to the fabric, making sure that any pattern on the fabric is straight and centred. Cut out the flag. Repeat until you have cut out a total of 26 flags in an assortment of fabrics.

3 **Put two flags** of different fabrics together so that you have a total of 13 mismatched pairs. Pin each pair together, wrong side to wrong side.

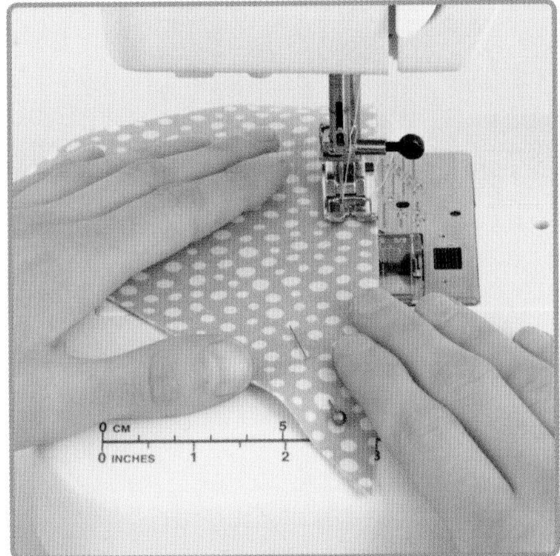

4 **Thread the machine** and bobbin with white thread. Using a straight stitch and leaving a 1cm (½in) seam allowance, stitch together the two long sides of each pair of flags. Repeat for all 13 pairs.

Measure 5cm (2in)
between each flag

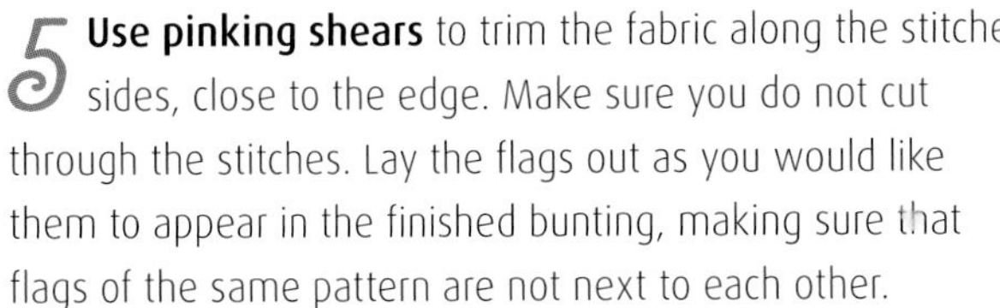

5 **Use pinking shears** to trim the fabric along the stitched sides, close to the edge. Make sure you do not cut through the stitches. Lay the flags out as you would like them to appear in the finished bunting, making sure that flags of the same pattern are not next to each other.

6 **Fold the bias binding** in half. Leaving 7.5cm (3in) of binding free at one end, insert the first flag inside the folded bias binding. Pin it in place, making sure the flag sits evenly against the fold in the binding. Measure 5cm (2in) from the end of the first flag, then pin the next flag in place. Repeat, working your way along the bias binding, until all 13 flags are pinned in place.

7 **Trim the other end** of the bias binding so 7.5cm (3in) remains free. Thread the machine and bobbin with thread that matches the bias binding. Starting at one end of the binding, carefully straight stitch along the unfolded edge, sewing the flags in place and the folded bias binding together. Remove the pins as you work.

Luxury soap

Sunny days bonnet

Crocheted jewellery

Tin can cacti planters

Stencilled beach bags

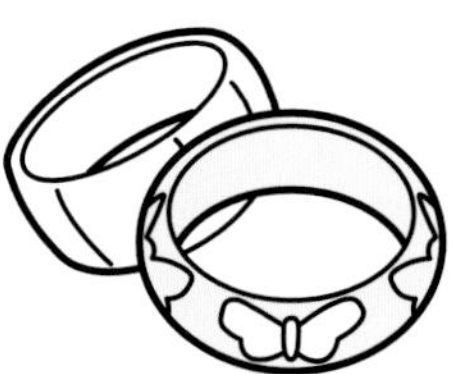

Découpage bangle

Quilted sewing set

Raspberry jam

Mosaic flowerpots

SUMMER

Tabletop water garden

Crocheted flowers

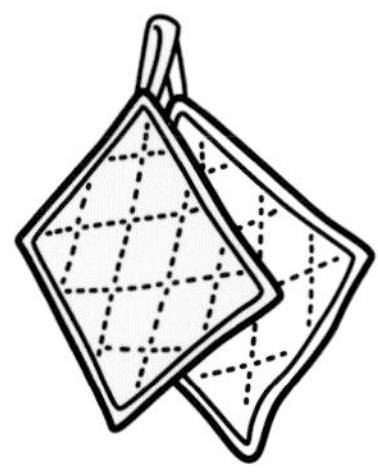
Quilted pot holder

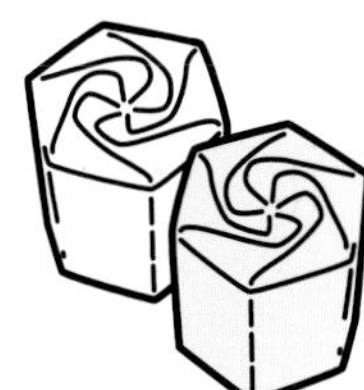
Twist-top gift box

LUXURY SOAP

Handmade soaps make indulgent gifts, and with the melt-and-pour method require no specialist skill to make. Create naturally scented and coloured soaps using spices, dried fruit or flowers, essential oils, and natural mineral dyes.

HOW TO MAKE LUXURY SOAP

Materials

* Gloves
* Knife
* 1kg (2¼lb) white melt-and-pour soap bars
* Heatproof bowl
* Pan
* Spatula
* Spoon
* ¼–¾ tsp yellow natural mineral colour
* Dried lemon peel granules
* Lemon essential oil
* Square mould
* Surgical spirit in a spray bottle
* 9 dried lemon slices
* Clingfilm

1 **Wearing gloves**, chop the melt-and-pour soap into pieces and heat in a heatproof bowl over a pan of boiling water, stirring occasionally, until all lumps have melted.

2 **Add the desired** amount of colouring to the melted soap base and stir until the powder has mixed in and the colour is evenly distributed.

3 **Add the lemon peel granules** a little at a time, stirring gently. Continue stirring until the granules are spread evenly throughout the soap mixture.

4 **Just before you pour** the soap mixture into the mould, slowly add the essential oil and stir gently until it is evenly distributed throughout.

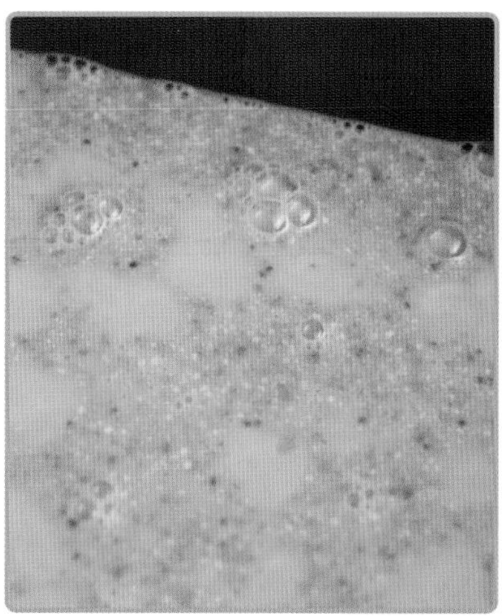

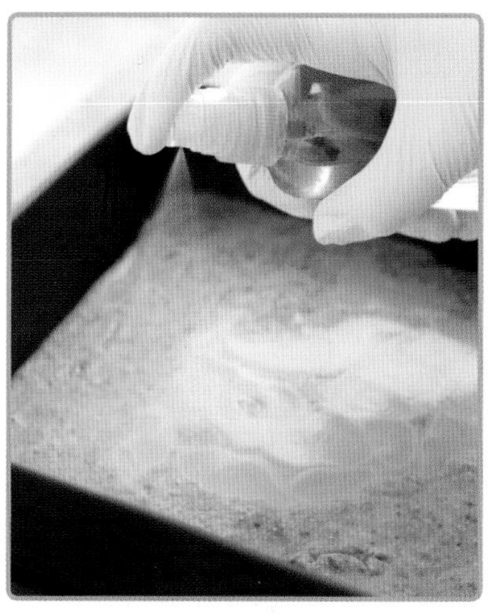

5 **Pour approximately** three-quarters of the mixture into the mould. Leave the remainder in the bowl over the hot water to keep it melted and warm.

6 **Spray the mixture** with surgical spirit to remove any bubbles. Leave this first layer for 20–25 minutes until it is almost set. It should be hard but warm.

7 **Spray the almost-set** layer again with surgical spirit. This will act as a glue and help it to bond to the next layer of soap.

8 **Slowly pour** the remaining mixture into the mould and add the dried lemon slices. You will need to act fast, as the top layer will begin to set as soon as it is poured in.

9 **Create a 3 x 3 pattern** so that each slice of soap will contain a lemon slice. Spritz the surface with surgical spirit to remove any bubbles and leave until hard.

10 **Remove the soap** from the mould and cut it with a knife into nine even squares. Wrap each square in clingfilm to prevent it attracting moisture.

OTHER IDEAS

Juniper cake-slice soap

You will need:

* 1kg (2 1/4lb) white melt-and-pour soap base
* 1/4 tsp pink natural mineral colour
* 2 1/2 tsp juniper essential oil
* 100g (3 1/2oz) juniper berries

This soap cake is made like the lemon soap on pp.60–61, but in two stages. First, melt half the soap, adding the pink colour and half the essential oil. Pour it into a round container and let it set, spritzing it with surgical spirit to get rid of any bubbles. Melt the second half of the soap, adding the remaining scent. Spritz the base again, and pour on the second layer of soap. Add the juniper berries to the top, spritzing it one final time to get rid of any remaining bubbles. Once set, remove from the mould and cut into slices.

Moulded vanilla stars

You will need:

* 1kg (2 1/4lb) white melt-and-pour soap base
* 1/4–3/4 tsp cream natural mineral colour
* 2 1/2 tsp vanilla essential oil
* 30g (1oz) vanilla pods

These vanilla-scented stars are made in the same way as the lemon soap on pp.60–61, but the mixture is poured into individual moulds to set. Soap moulds are sold in craft shops, or you could use silicone cake moulds. Vanilla seeds are used instead of lemon peel granules as an exfoliant and for added scent. Vanilla pods can also be used to decorate the tops of the stars by placing them into the mould before the mixture is poured on top.

Cookie-cutter lavender hearts

You will need:

* 1kg (2¼lb) white melt-and-pour soap base
* ¼–¾ tsp purple natural mineral colour
* 2½ tsp lavender essential oil
* 10g (¼oz) dried lavender

These heart-shaped soaps are made using the same method and quantity of ingredients as the Lemon soap on pp.60–61, swapping in the ingredients above. However, instead of cutting the soap into squares, they are cut with heart-shaped cookie cutters. The lavender buds will float to the top, creating an exfoliating layer.

See-through orange soap

You will need:

* 1kg (2¼lb) clear melt-and-pour soap base
* 2½ tsp bergamot essential oil
* 9 dried orange slices

Made in the same way as the lemon soap on pp.60–61, using a clear soap base and adding a dried orange slice inside the soap gives these soaps a fresh look. Make them by melting half of the clear soap base, and adding half of the essential oil. Pour the mixture into a square mould, and add the orange slices to the top. Allow to set before melting the remaining half of the soap base and adding the remaining oil. Spritz the set layer with surgical spirit and add the melted soap mixture to the top. Spritz again to get rid of any bubbles and allow to set. Cut the into nine squares.

SUNNY DAYS BONNET

Perfect for sunny days in the garden or for a picnic, this cloth sun bonnet will fit a baby aged 9–12 months. Choose bright fabrics that complement one another.

HOW TO MAKE A CLOTH SUN BONNET

Materials

* Tracing or tissue paper
* Pencil
* Scissors
* Pins
* 48.5 x 58.5cm (19 x 23in) cotton main fabric
* 48.5 x 51cm (19 x 20in) cotton lining fabric
* 18 x 35.5cm (7 x 14in) fusible interfacing
* Iron
* Sewing machine
* Matching thread
* 25.5cm (10in) of 1cm (½in) elastic
* Two safety pins

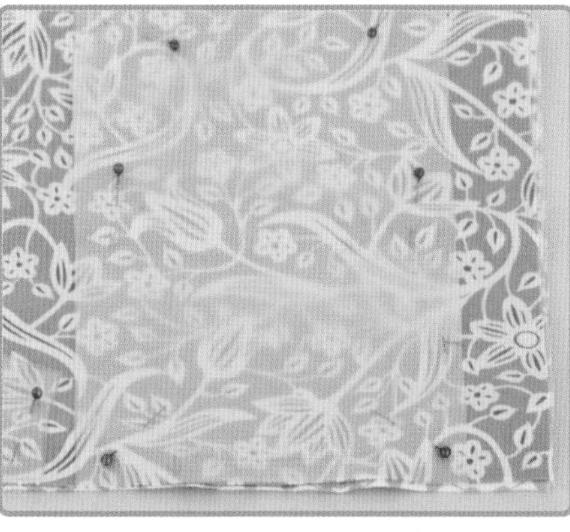

1 **Trace the pattern templates** on page 69 onto tracing or tissue paper and cut them out. Pin the pattern pieces to the fabrics and interfacing, as specified on the pattern. Cut them out.

2 **Iron interfacing** to the wrong side of the brim main fabric and to the brim lining fabric, making sure the interfacing is shiny side down. Follow the instructions that come with your interfacing when ironing it to the fabric.

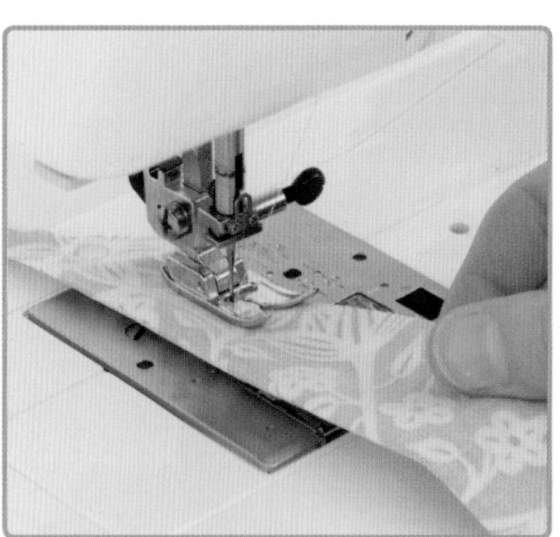

3 **Fold and pin** the tie band pieces lengthways, right side to right side, as indicated on the pattern. Leaving a 1cm (½in) seam allowance, sew along the angled ends and long sides. Turn to the right side, then iron.

4 **Place the interfaced** brim pieces right side to right side and stitch around the edge, leaving a 1cm (½in) seam allowance. Trim and clip the curves, then turn to the right side and iron.

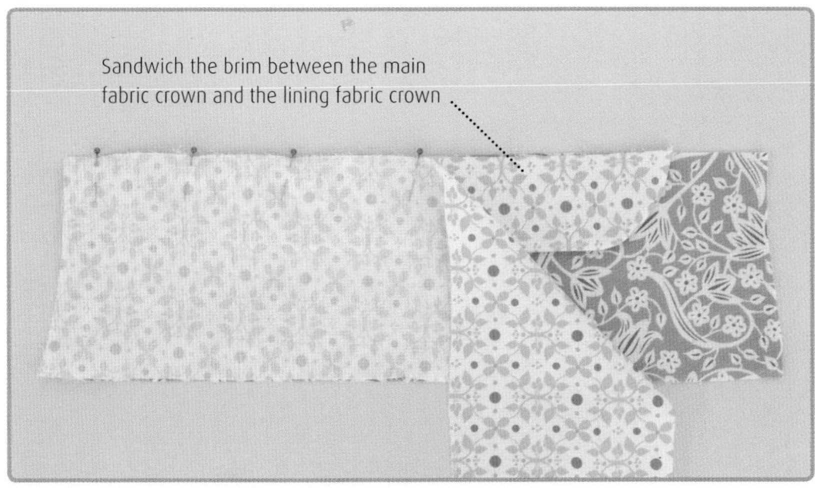

Sandwich the brim between the main fabric crown and the lining fabric crown

5 **Place the brim on the edge** of the main fabric crown, right side to right side and matching the centres. Put the lining fabric crown on top, matching the front edges and sandwiching the brim in between. Stitch along the edge, through all the layers, then turn through to the right side and iron.

6 **Matching the markings** on the pattern, pin the main fabric back to the free edge of the main fabric crown, right side to right side. Make 5mm (¼in) snips along the curved edge.

7 **Sew along the pinned curved** edge leaving a 1cm (½in) seam allowance. Iron the seam towards the centre of the bonnet. Repeat steps 6 and 7 to join the lining back to the lining crown. Turn the bonnet right side out.

8 **Join the bottom edge** of the back by pinning the free edges of the main and lining backs together, matching the seams. Stitch along the entire length.

9 **Pin the tie bands** to the two front corners below the brim, 5mm (¼in) from the bottom edge. Position them so they stick outwards, as shown. Stitch them in place.

10 **Fold up the bottom** edge 2cm (¾in) towards the lining of the bonnet, then fold it up again by the same amount. Pin in place.

Topstitch
along the
folded edge

11 **To form the** casing for the elastic, topstitch close to the edge of the first fold you made, removing the pins as you work.

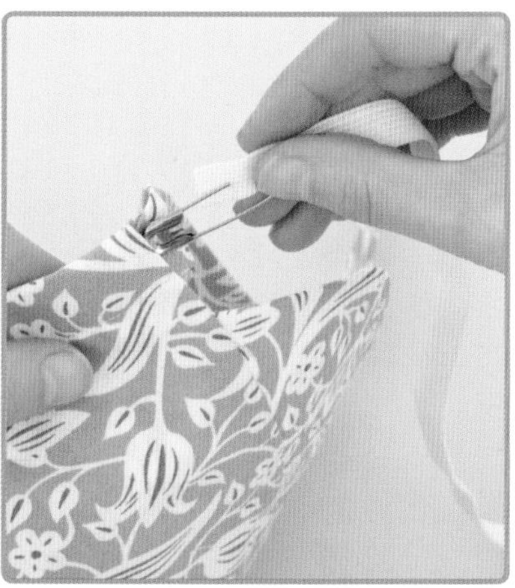

12 **With a safety pin on each end** of the elastic, thread it through the casing, so that the ends are just out of sight inside the casing.

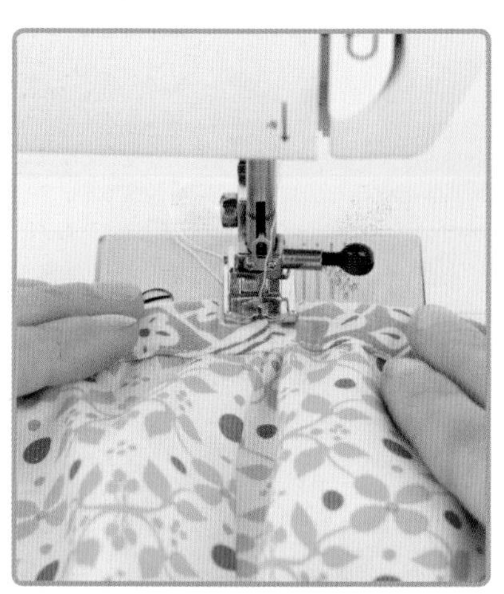

13 **Topstitch across the casing** over the seam where the back joins the crown on one side only: this will secure the elastic in place on that side of the bonnet.

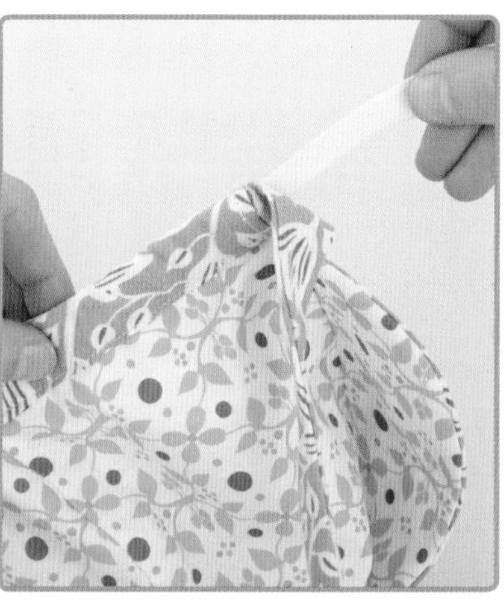

14 **Pull the other end** of the elastic to gather the fabric at the back of the bonnet. Sew across the casing over the other seam where the back joins the crown to secure the elastic in place on this side of the bonnet, as in step 13. Each end of the elastic will still have a safety pin attached to it.

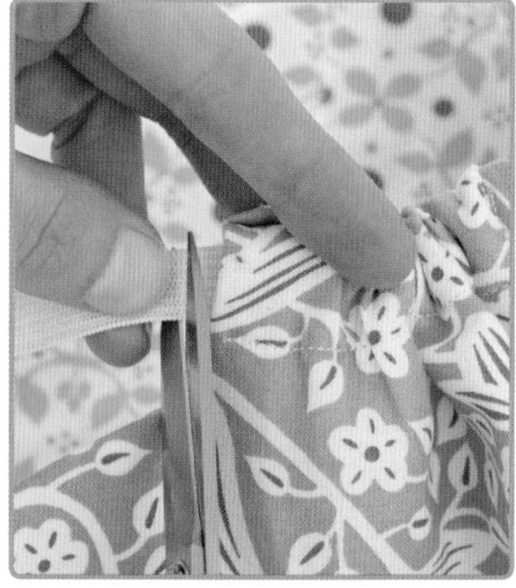

15 **Pull on one of the safety pins** to pull the end of the elastic out of the casing. Cut the elastic as short as you can. The remaining elastic will spring back into the casing and no longer be visible. Repeat on the other side of the bonnet.

TEMPLATES

Template

Enlarge by 225% on a photocopier

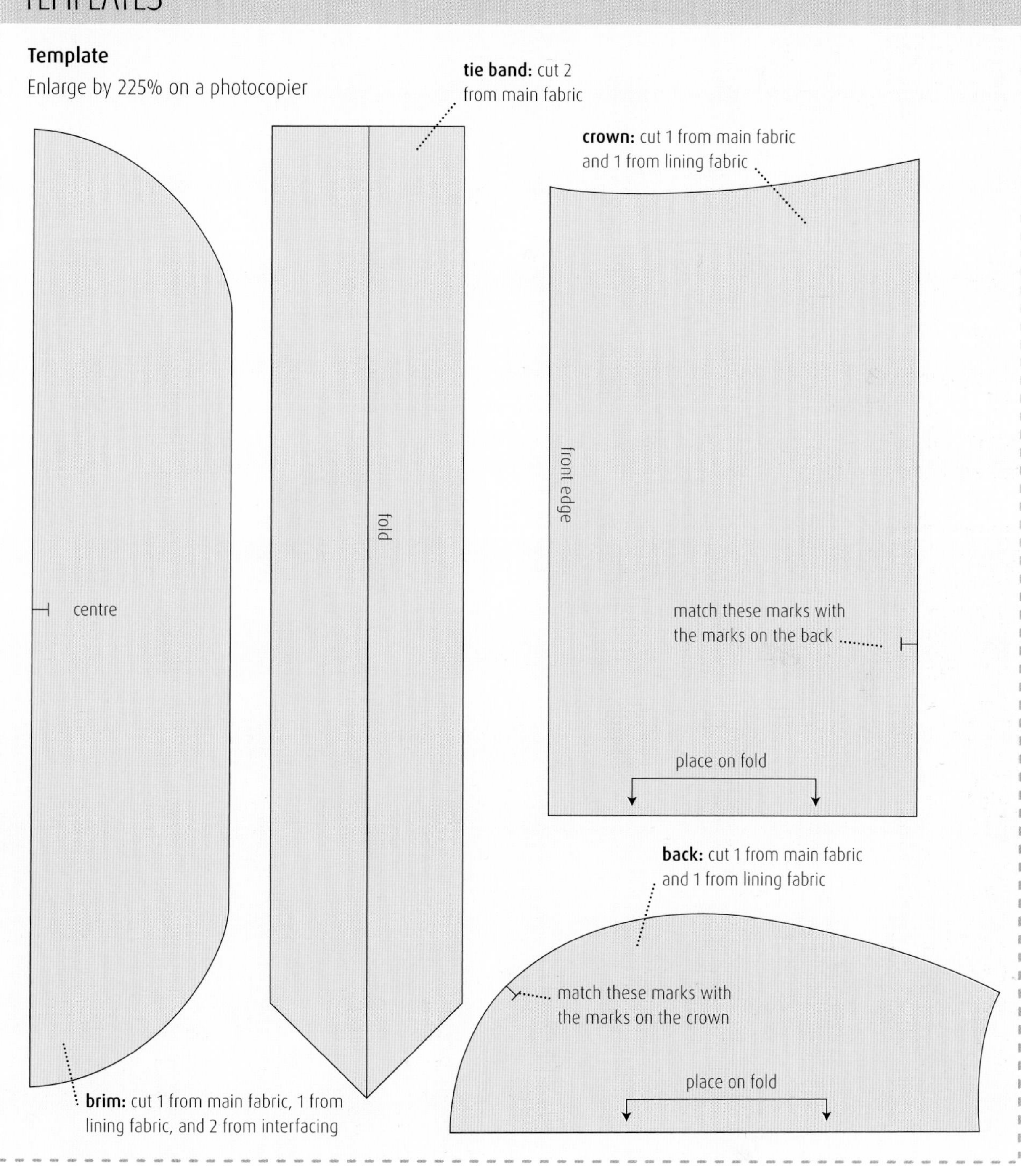

CROCHETED JEWELLERY

Create a bracelet with simple charm. Work the chain to a length that fits comfortably around your wrist once for a short bracelet, or multiply this by as many times as you want for a longer, thicker-looking bracelet.

HOW TO MAKE CROCHETED JEWELLERY

Materials

FOR THE CHUNKY BRACELET

Use any small amounts of DK yarn for this project, or try different weights – the chain will simply get thicker or thinner depending on the weight of the yarn.

x 1

* 3.5mm crochet hook
* Yarn needle
* Approx 1cm (½in) button or bead for fastening

FOR THE BEADED NECKLACE

Use any yarn for this project – it only uses a very small amount so is perfect for using up scraps. The chain will simply get thicker or thinner – just make sure that the thread can fit through the holes of the beads you have chosen

x 1

* 2mm crochet hook
* 1.5mm beading hook, or size needed to fit through your beads
* Yarn needle
* Selection of beads

CHUNKY BRACELET

NOTE Increasing the number of strands of yarn you hold together to crochet with will vary the bracelet's thickness.

Pattern

With a single strand of yarn, make a chain to your desired length, plus 5 ch. Ss into fifth ch from hook. Fasten off yarn, weave in ends.

2-strand variation

With 2 strands of yarn, make a chain to your desired length, plus 4 ch. Ss into fourth ch from hook. Fasten off yarn, weave in ends.

3-strand variation

With 3 strands of yarn, make a chain to your desired length, plus 3 ch. Ss into third ch from hook. Fasten off yarn, weave in ends.

Finishing

Sew a bead or button to the opposite end from the loop fastening.

1 **When the chain** is the desired length, make a loop by working an extra 5 chains and then make a slip stitch into the fifth chain from the hook.

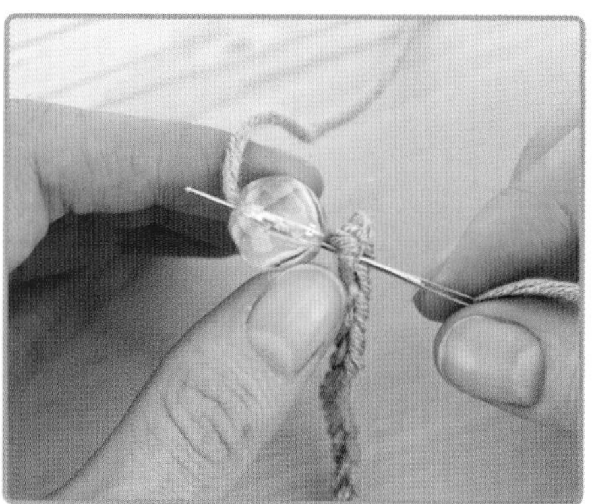

2 **Attach a bead** or button securely to the opposite end from the loop using the same yarn, and then weave in loose ends.

BEADED NECKLACE

NOTE To thread the beads onto the chain, you need to ensure that the beading hook can pass through the holes in the beads, so don't choose any beads with tiny holes.

Pattern

Make a chain of the desired length to your first bead placement.
Pull up the loop on the hook to make it larger and remove the hook from the loop.
Place a bead onto the shaft of the beading hook, then insert the hook into the elongated loop.
Pull the loop through the bead and work 1 ch to secure it, pulling on the yarn to make sure that the yarn is tight around the bead.
Repeat these actions at intervals to place all the beads desired.
Work a length of chain after the last bead has been placed, and join this with a ss to the first chain made on the necklace to form a ring and complete the necklace.
Fasten off yarn, weave in ends.

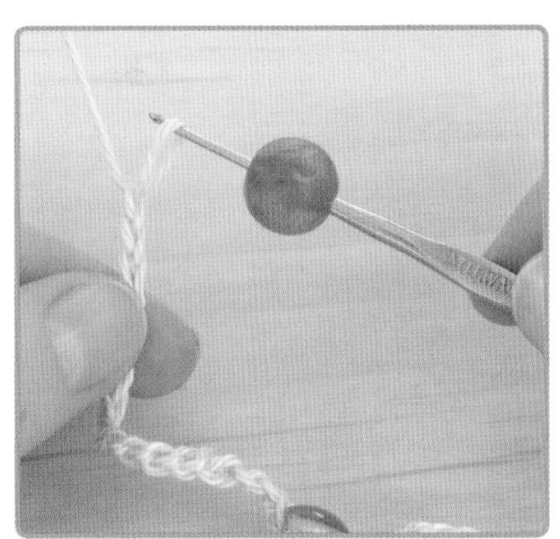

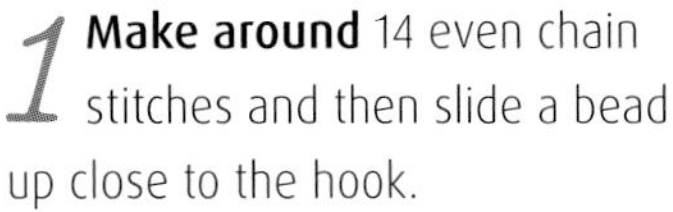

1 **Make around** 14 even chain stitches and then slide a bead up close to the hook.

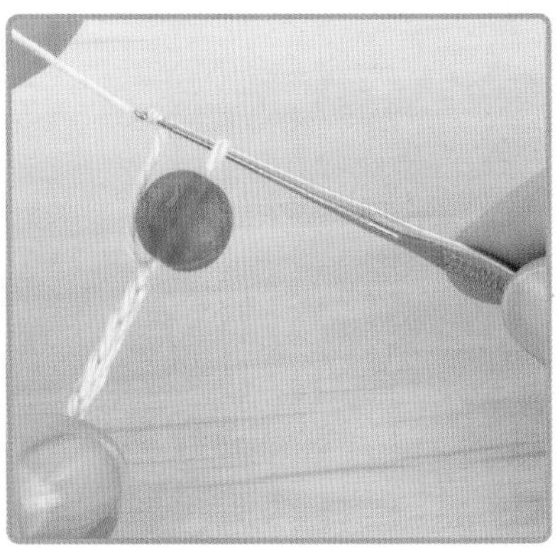

2 **Thread the bead** onto the yarn and make a chain stitch tightly around the bead to secure it in position on the necklace.

TIN CAN CACTI PLANTERS

For a taste of Mexico without leaving your garden, create a desert scene with architectural cacti and juicy succulents grouped together in bright food tins for a brilliant table display.

La Chinata
INGREDIENTS : GRAINS DE POIVRE VERT - EAU - SEL
INGREDIENTS : GREEN PEPPERCORNS WATER - SALT
Pimentón de la Vera
Denomination of Origin Protected
SANTO DOMINGO
ACEITE de OLIVA

HOW TO MAKE A TIN CAN PLANTER

Materials

- Collection of tin cans with appealing designs printed onto the metal
- Masking tape
- Electric drill & drill bits
- Hydroleca or gravel
- John Innes No. 2 potting compost
- Horticultural grit
- Dibber, chopstick, or pencil
- Decorative gravel

Plant list

- *Aloe aristata*
- *Aloe brevifolia*
- *Chamaelobivia* 'Kawinai'
- *Chamaelobivia* 'Rose Quartz'
- *Echeveria agavoides* 'Red Edge'
- *Haworthia glauca* var. *herrei f. jacobseniana*
- *Pachyphytum hookeri*
- *Rebutia* species
- *Sedum* 'Spiral Staircase'
- *Stenocereus dumortieri*

1 **Clean the tin cans** thoroughly before using. Drill drainage holes in the bottom of each can with an electric drill. Use masking tape to prevent the drill slipping.

2 **Add a layer** of drainage material, such as hydroleca or gravel, to the bottom of each can. Good drainage is vital so that the roots don't sit in water and rot.

3 **Mix up a free-draining** gritty compost from John Innes No. 2 and horticultural grit in 3:1 proportions. Remove plants from their pots and gently break up the root ball, teasing out the roots and removing soil. Take care not to damage the roots.

4 **Place plants** on a layer of compost and then fill in around the root ball, working in the compost with a dibber to reduce air pockets. Tap the container on the work surface to distribute the compost evenly. Top with a layer of decorative gravel. Place on a saucer or similar if you need to protect the table surface.

5 **Repot plants** into large containers when roots start to show through the tin's drainage hole. Repotting is best done in spring, and watering plants a couple of days before keeps roots moist.

CARE ADVICE

WHERE TO SITE

Cacti and succulents need a sunny site and warmth to thrive. You can leave them outside in summer, as long as there is adequate protection and shelter from rain. Bring inside during winter and place on a sunny windowsill in a warm room.

WATERING AND FEEDING

The easiest way to water these is to place the tins in a shallow container of water, leave until the surface of the compost is moist, then lift out and leave to drain. Water regularly in the growing season – every 10 days or so – and add a diluted liquid feed to the water during spring and summer. Do not feed or water in autumn and winter.

STENCILLED BEACH BAGS

Turn plain canvas bags into unique and personal fashion statements with the use of paper stencils and fabric paint. Once you can stencil with confidence, why not try decorating a T-shirt or cushion cover?

HOW TO MAKE BEACH BAGS

Materials

* Pencil
* Tracing paper
* Stencil paper or card
* Scalpel
* Cutting mat
* Fabric bag
* Iron
* Scrap paper or newspaper
* Masking tape
* Fabric paint in two colours
* Plate or palette
* Sponge
* Hairdryer
* Kitchen towel

1 **Draw a design of your choice** onto tracing paper. Transfer it onto card by flipping the tracing paper over and drawing over the lines while pressing down firmly.

2 **Use a scalpel** to carefully cut the stencil shape out. If making a repeat pattern, you can cut out the stencil shape a number of times on one sheet, making sure to leave a border of paper.

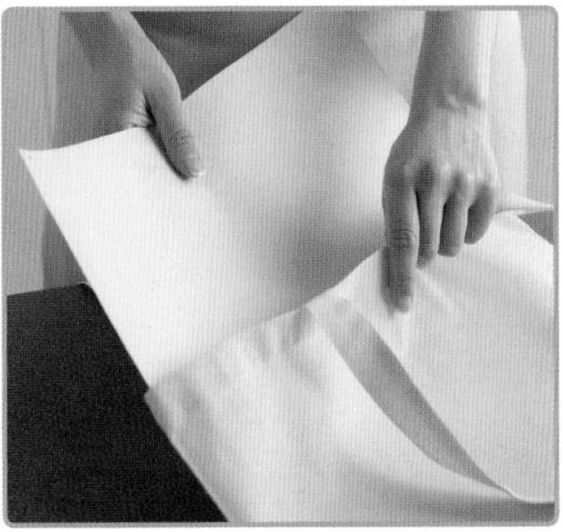

3 **Prepare your fabric bag** by ironing it, and line the inside with scrap paper or newspaper to stop any excess ink that may soak through the fabric from running through to the back of the bag.

4 **Tape down the stencil**. Pour some paint on a plate or palette. Dip a clean, dry sponge in the paint, dabbing off any excess. Then apply the paint with the sponge, starting from the centre and working out.

5 **Remove your stencil** and put it to one side to dry. Use a hairdryer to dry the paint onto the fabric, ensuring you blow dry the inside of your fabric bag as well as the front so the paint doesn't dry to the lining paper.

6 **Use kitchen towel** to blot your stencil and let it dry. You can also prepare more stencils, allowing you to move on with the design while you wait for the first stencil to dry.

7 **Once your stencil** and fabric paint are dry, reposition your stencil on the bag. Repeat the application process as many times as desired, leaving a few gaps for the second colour.

8 **Once you've stencilled** all of the design in one colour and it has dried, apply the second colour in the same way as the first, using a new stencil. Leave to dry overnight.

9 **When the fabric paint** has fully dried, iron the fabric for a minute or two to fix the paint to the material. You may wish to use a cloth to protect your iron.

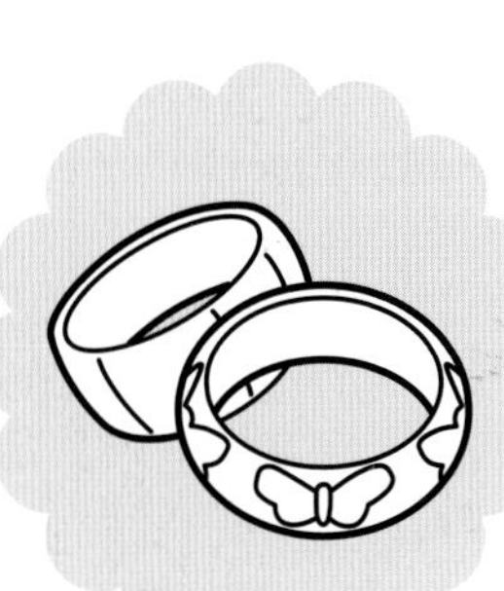

DÉCOUPAGE BANGLE

To make these stylish bangle bracelets, paper cut-outs are glued down and varnished to create a smooth, shiny surface. Almost any paper can be used for this technique, making these bangles the ultimate bespoke gift.

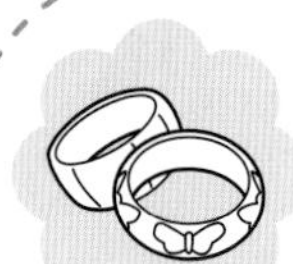

HOW TO MAKE A DÉCOUPAGE BANGLE

Materials

* Ruler
* Bangle (wooden or plastic)
* Scissors
* Craft glue
* Solid, coloured or patterned backing paper
* Decorative paper motifs
* White tack
* Paintbrushes
* Craft paint
* Glitter (optional)
* Clear varnish

1 **Measure the distance** around the side of the bangle. Cut paper strips, 1.5cm (⅝in) wide and long enough to wrap around the bangle. Cut enough strips to cover the bangle.

2 **Spread glue all over** the back of one paper strip, but don't soak it. Position the strip around the edge of the bangle so that the ends overlap on the inside. Remove any air.

3 **Continue adding strips**, overlapping slightly with each previous strip, until you have covered the bangle completely with the backing paper.

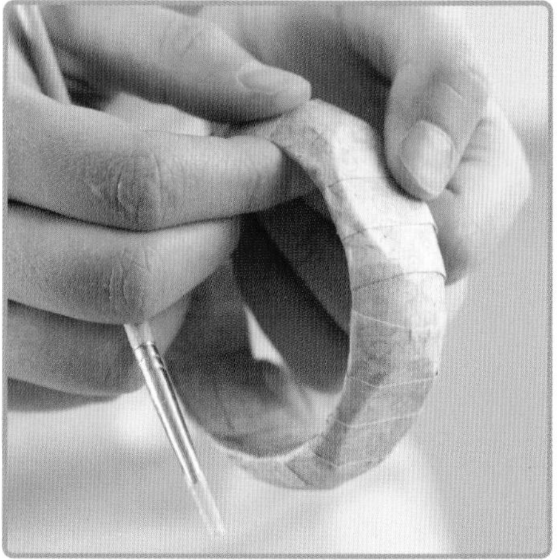

4 **When you have finished** this stage, check that each strip of paper is firmly glued down. Smooth out any bumps or wrinkles, adding more glue as necessary.

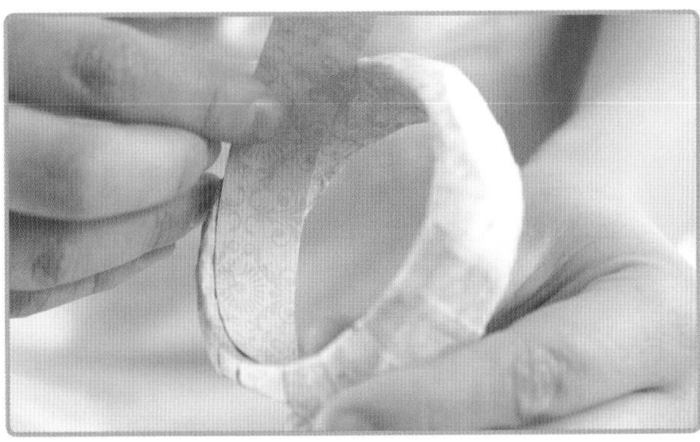

5 **Cut another strip** of the backing paper for the inside of the bangle. This will need to cover the entire inside surface for a neat finish. Glue in place and leave to dry.

6 **Carefully cut out** the motifs. Position them around the bangle using white tack, moving them around until you have decided on a design that works for you.

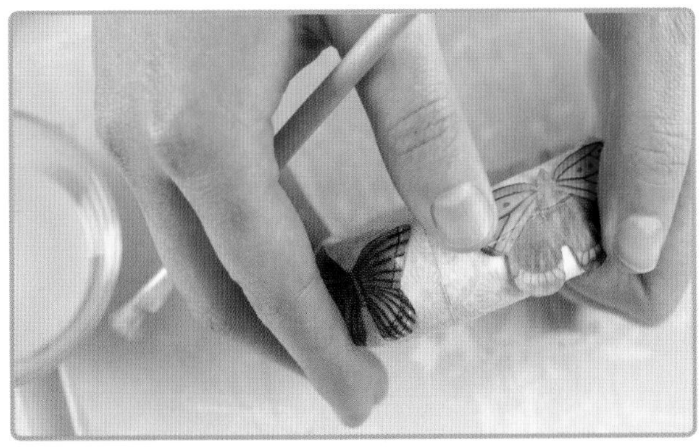

7 **Glue the motifs** onto the bangle. Take care when sticking down the motifs as they are likely to tear easily when wet with glue, and will be difficult to reposition.

8 **Paint a thin border** around the top edge of the bangle; leave to dry. Turn the bangle around and paint the other edge. Add glitter, if desired, and leave to dry.

9 **Varnish the bangle** and leave to dry for two to three days, turning occasionally. When hardened, repeat with a second coat of varnish. Leave to dry as before.

QUILTED SEWING SET

Keep your needles safely stored, tidy, and easily transportable in these cute quilting projects. The book protects the needles and the cushion makes them readily accessible.

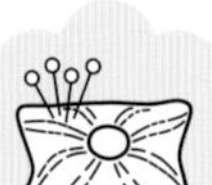

MAKING A QUILTED SEWING SET

Materials

FOR BOTH PROJECTS

* Threads to match your fabrics
* Sewing machine
* Pins
* Scissors
* Iron & ironing board
* Sewing needle

FOR NEEDLE BOOK

* Nine 5 x 5cm (2 x 2in) pieces of coordinating fabrics with different prints
* 11 x 11cm (4½ x 4½in) back cover fabric
* 11 x 22.5cm (4½ x 9in) lining fabric
* 7.6cm (3in) elastic cord
* 10 x 20cm (4 x 8in) wadding
* 9.5 x 9.5cm (3¾ x 3¾in) felt, or aida cloth
* Thread to match your felt
* 2cm (¾in) self-covered button in a coordinating fabric

NEEDLE BOOK

(SEE P87 FOR PICTURE)

Make the front cover

Arrange the coordinating fabrics in a nine-patch arrangement of your choice. With right sides together, stitch the three patches in each row together, then join the top, middle, and bottom rows. Press the seams. This forms the front cover of the needle book.

Join the front and back

Lay the front cover on top of the back cover fabric, right sides together. Pin along the edge that is to be the spine, then sew together to join the front and back covers. Open up and press the seam open.

Add the lining and the elastic

Lay the joined front and back covers on top of the lining fabric, right sides together. Fold the piece of elastic in half to create a loop. Place the loop between the back cover and the lining fabric, half way along the short side. The raw ends of the elastic should stick out of the side of the book by about 6mm (¼in) and the loop should sit between the two layers of fabric. Pin the elastic in place, then pin around all four sides of the book.

Sew the sides and turn through

Sew around all four sides, leaving a 5cm (2in) gap along one long side. Sew over the ends of the elastic to secure in place. Snip off the four corners, taking care not to cut through the stitches. Turn the needle book to the right side through the gap. Carefully pull out all the corners with a pin, then iron.

Insert the wadding

Insert the piece of wadding inside the book through the gap in the stitches. Make sure it lies flat and even, then hand sew the gap closed. If you want to quilt your needle book, do it at this stage, before adding the felt page.

Attach the felt page

Place the piece of felt so that one of its edges sits at the centre fold of the book. Pin in place along this edge. Using a matching top thread and a bobbin thread that matches the back cover fabric, topstitch along the edge, leaving a 2mm ($^{1}/_{16}$in) seam allowance.

Stitch on the button

Position the button on the front cover so it aligns with the elastic loop. Sew it in place, only catching the front cover fabric so the stitches are not visible on the other side.

PIN CUSHION

Make the front

With fabric A right side down, centre the card template on top of the fabric. Either finger press or use an iron to press the sides of the fabric over the template, starting by folding over the corners. Continue folding over and pressing the fabric over the card. Remove the card and press again. Find the centre of the fabric by folding the square in half and pressing the fold. Repeat again in the opposite direction and press lightly. With the fabric still right side down, fold up and press each corner of the square to the centre mark on the fabric. Press all sides. Catch stitch the four corner points in place. Repeat the folding process again on the four sides, pressing the creases but not stitching them in place.

Open up the four triangular flaps and place fabric B, right side up, on the plain fabric, using the creases as a guide. Fold the triangular flaps in so the points meet in the centre. Pin all four outside corners and pin the four points in the centre, then anchor the points in the centre through all the layers with a few cross stitches.

Pin the four half-square fabric C triangles right side up to each of the triangular flaps, 3mm (⅛in) inside the edge of fabric A. Roll the edge of fabric A over fabric C, curving fabric A so the rolled edge is wider in the middle and narrower at each end, forming a "petal" shape. Pin as required. Repeat on the remaining seven edges. Increase the stitch size on your machine slightly, then top stitch along the rolled edge, beginning in the centre. Repeat for the seven remaining curves.

Make the back

On the reverse of one fabric D rectangle, measure 4cm (1½in) down along one long edge. Rotate the rectangle 180 degrees and repeat on the other side. Place the second rectangle under the first, right sides together and, leaving a 6mm (¼in) seam allowance, stitch to the mark, backstitching to finish. Rotate and stitch to the mark again, leaving a gap of approximately 4cm (1½in). Finger press the seam open.

Place the front and back of the cushion right sides together. Align and pin the edges in place. Stitch around the four sides, then trim off the excess fabric so the raw edges are neat. Gently turn the cushion through the opening in the back seam, pushing out the corners.

Stuff and button the cushion

Stuff the cushion and oversew the gap in the back by hand. Stitch the shanked button to the front of the cushion with double thread, passing the needle through to the back and through the washer button. Pull the thread to compress the pin cushion and tie the thread off securely.

Materials

FOR BOTH PROJECTS

* Threads to match your fabrics
* Iron & ironing board
* Sewing needle
* Pins
* Sewing machine
* Scissors

FOR PIN CUSHION

* 22 x 22cm (8½ x 8½in) thin card template
* 26.5 x 26.5cm (10½ x 10½in) square of plain teal-coloured
* 11 x 11cm (4½ x 4½in) square of red fabric
* 10 x 20cm (4 x 8in) piece of patterned teal-coloured fabric, cut and made into four half-square triangles
* Two 7.5 x 15cm (3 x 6in) rectangles of the same patterned teal-coloured fabric, for the back
* Toy filling or wadding
* 2.5cm (1in) button with shank, covered in fabric C
* 1.5cm (⅝in) plain flat button for the back, used as a washer

RASPBERRY JAM

Homemade jam has a delicious depth of flavour and fruity freshness that you won't find in shop-bought produce.

HOW TO MAKE RASPBERRY JAM

Makes 2 small jars

Ingredients

* 650g ($1^1/_2$lb) raspberries (preferably not overripe)
* Juice of $^1/_2$ lemon
* 75g ($2^1/_2$oz) granulated sugar

Equipment

* Preserving pan or large, heavy-based saucepan
* Large wooden spoon
* Sterilized wide-mouthed jam funnel (optional)
* Ladle
* Sterilized jars with metal lids or cellophane covers and elastic bands
* Skimmer or slotted spoon (optional)
* Discs of waxed paper

1 **Put a few small saucers** in the fridge to chill. Place the fruit in a preserving pan or large heavy-based saucepan. Add the lemon juice and 150ml (5fl oz) of water. The lemon juice provides extra acid, which is vital for setting, as raspberries tend to be low in acid.

2 **Simmer the fruit** gently for 3–5 minutes to soften and release its juices. Then add the sugar and stir it in over a gentle heat. Once it has all dissolved, turn the heat to high. Remember sugar inhibits the release of pectin and toughens the skins of fruits, so always add it to the pan after the fruit has softened sufficiently.

3 **Bring the jam** to a rolling boil for 5–10 minutes or until the setting point is reached. Start testing for the setting point when the bubbles in the jam become large and start "plopping".

4 **Take the pan off the heat** to test for a set. Put one teaspoon of jam on one of the cold saucers. Leave it to cool, then push it to one side with your finger. If it wrinkles and your finger leaves a trail, it is set.

5 **Ladle the jam into** warm sterilized jars using a sterilized jam funnel. Fill the jars almost to the brim. Cover the hot jam with waxed paper discs and seal with metal lids, or cellophane covers and elastic bands. If there is scum on the surface of the jam, use a skimmer to remove it before you pot up, or stir the jam in the same direction until the scum has dispersed.

VARIATION

Plum and port jam

Makes 6 medium jars

Put 1.8kg (4lb) dark plums, a cinnamon stick, and the juice of one lime in a preserving pan or a large, heavy-bottomed saucepan and add 600ml (1 pint) of water. Bring the fruit mix to a simmering point. Turn the heat down to low just as it starts to bubble, then simmer for 15–20 minutes or until the plums begin to break down and soften. Add 1.35kg (3lb) granulated sugar, stirring with a wooden spoon until completely dissolved. Turn the heat up high, bring to the boil, and keep at a rolling boil for 5–8 minutes or until the mixture thickens and the bubbles become large and start "plopping". Test for a set using the wrinkle test (see Step 4). If the jam hasn't set, bring it back to a rolling boil for another minute and test again. When the jam has set, carefully remove the cinnamon stick, stir in 2–3 tablespoons of port, then ladle the jam into warm sterilized jars. Cover with waxed paper discs, seal and leave to cool.

MOSAIC FLOWERPOTS

These mosaic flowerpots will bring an extra splash of colour to your garden. They are made up of fragments of broken china and unglazed ceramic tiles.

HOW TO MAKE MOSAIC FLOWERPOTS

Materials

* China plates
* Towel
* Hammer
* Tile nippers
* Terracotta pot approx 15cm (6in) high
* 70:30 solution of washable PVA glue and water
* Medium-size paintbrush
* Pencil
* Unglazed glass mosaic tiles
* Cement-based adhesive
* Plasterer's small tool or palette knife
* White grout
* Sponge

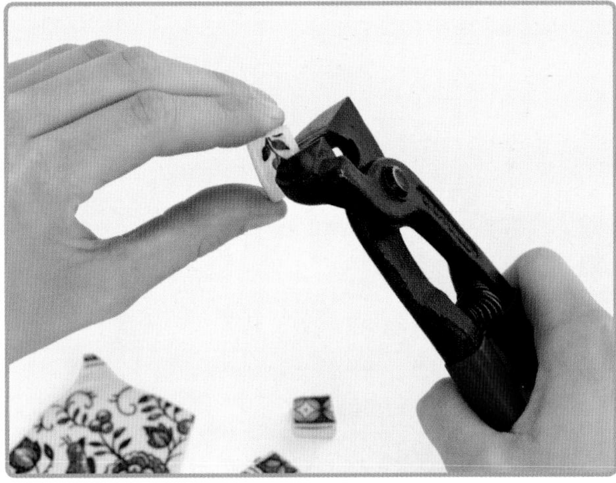

1 **Wrap the china plates** in a towel and smash them with a hammer. Cut the pieces into smaller, more regular shapes using tile nippers.

2 **Seal the terracotta pot** by painting it with the PVA solution and leave to dry.

3 **Draw a simple** design onto the pot in pencil and lay out the same motif on your work surface using the blue glass tiles. Cut these into strips to make the stem and into triangles for the flower and leaves.

4 **Apply cement-based adhesive** to the pot's surface with a plasterer's small tool or palette knife, roughly following the design. Position the blue tile pieces on the adhesive, starting with the flower.

5 **Fill in the background** with pieces of broken plate. Choose pieces with a similar pattern to make a border around the rim. Apply adhesive to small areas at a time, turning the pot upside down to reach the base more easily. When the adhesive is dry, grout the piece and wipe away excess grout with a damp sponge (see Techniques, below).

TECHNIQUES

Grouting

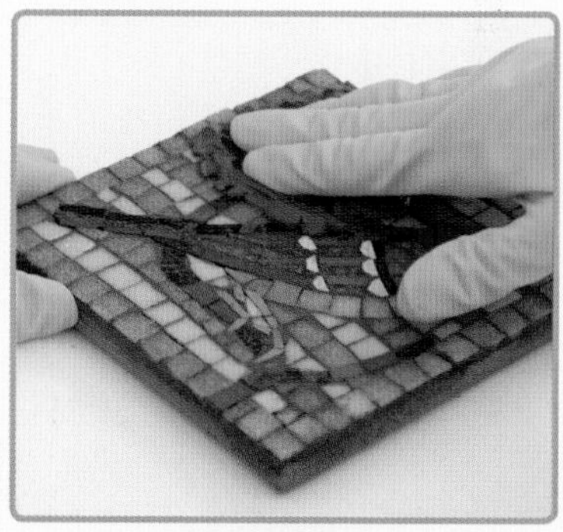

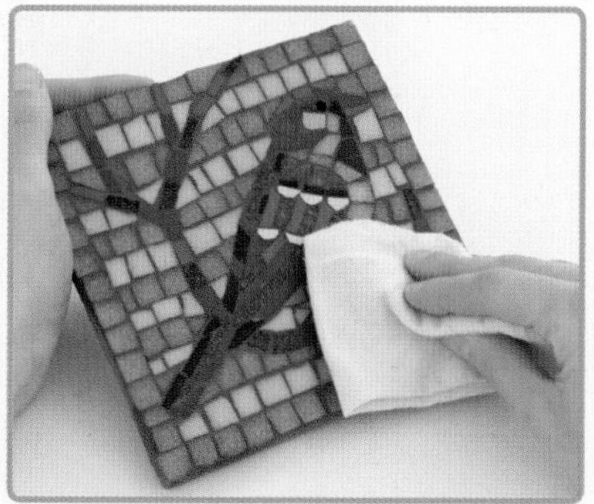

1 **Grout the front** of the mosaic to fill any gaps either immediately or after the adhesive has dried. Moisten the surface of the mosaic with a damp sponge, then spread grout across the surface, working it into the gaps. Clean with a damp sponge, turning the sponge with every wipe.

2 **After about 20 minutes**, when the grout has begun to dry, pass a dry cloth over the surface of the mosaic to remove any residual grout.

Removing excess grout

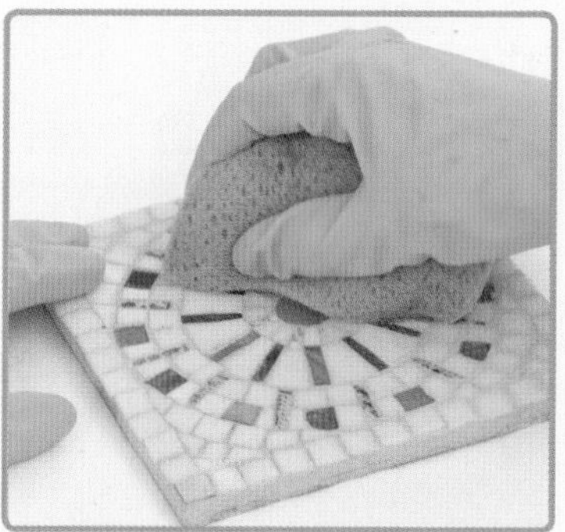

Clean off the excess grout with a damp sponge, turning the sponge over after every wipe so that you are always using a clean face. When the grout is almost dry, after about 20 minutes, clean off any surface residue with a dry cloth.

OTHER IDEAS

Owl jewellery box

You will need:

* Wooden box
* Glazed and unglazed ceramic tiles
* Glass nuggets and beads
* White grout
* Felt for the base

This pretty jewellery box is made using the same technique as the mosaic flowerpots on pp.96–97. Start by drawing a design of your choice on the box and then seal the box with watered-down PVA glue. Start filling in the design, attaching the nuggets and whole tiles first. Cut the remaining tiles to size to complete the design. Finally, fill in the area around the design with randomly cut tiles – a technique known as crazy paving. Allow to dry and then grout the lid. Grout the box one side at a time, waiting for each side to dry before starting the next. Glue felt to the base to finish the box.

Flower garland mirror

You will need:

* Mirror with wide, flat, wooden frame
* A selection of tiles and glass nuggets
* White grout

Make this mirror in the same way as the mosaic flowerpots on pp.96–97. Draw a design of your choice on the frame and seal with watered-down PVA glue. Create the flowers first, starting with a nugget and using tile nippers to shape the petals. Next, make the leaf garlands. Fill in the gaps with crazy paving and use tile halves to fill in the outer edge of the border. Cover the mirror with masking tape to protect it when grouting. Grout the frame, ensuring you create a straight edge around the mirror.

Round tea-light holder

You will need:

* Ball-shaped, wooden tea-light holder
* Old crockery, broken into small pieces
* Tiles and glass nuggets
* White grout
* Felt for the base

This tea-light holder is made in the same way as the mosaic flowerpots on pp.96–97, but using fragments of broken crockery. First, draw your design on the tea-light holder and then seal it with watered-down PVA glue. Glue down the nuggets first, and then use tile nippers to shape the crockery pieces into petals. Next, add any whole tiles. Finally, fill in the area around the design with more crockery pieces. Work a small area at a time. Some tiles may have to be held in place using tape until they dry. Grout, allow to dry, and attach felt to the base to finish.

Seaside coasters

You will need:

* MDF squares
* Tiles in a variety of colours
* Grey grout

These seaside-inspired coasters have been made out of squares of MDF, using the technique described for the mosaic flowerpots on pp.96–97. Using your own design, first draw guidelines onto the coaster in pencil. Fill in the design first, shaping the tiles to fit. Try to keep the tiles fairly flat, as you will need to be able to rest a glass or mug on the coaster when finished. Next, fill in the background using square tiles, shaping them to fit as necessary. Again, try to keep the tiles as flat as possible. Grout the coasters, not forgetting the edges, to finish.

TABLETOP WATER GARDEN

This little container garden means you can enjoy a water feature in the smallest of spaces. Ask your aquatics supplier for advice on plants suitable for smaller containers and shallow depths of water.

MAKING A TABLETOP WATER GARDEN

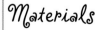

Materials

* Selection of aquarium gravel in contrasting colours & sizes
* Large, transparent glass or plastic bowl
* Selection of pebbles
* Smaller bowl or other container

* Rainwater or distilled water
* Shells

Plant list

* *Eichhornia crassipes*
* *Eleocharis acicularis*
* *Equisetum japonicum*
* *Sisyrinchium angustifolium*

1 **Carefully take plants** out of their pots and remove as much soil as you can while minimizing any damage to the roots.

2 **To loosen the soil** and make it easier to remove, you can also soak the plants in room temperature water.

3 **Keeping them separate**, thoroughly wash the gravels to remove any mud. Add one type of gravel to the large bowl. Build it up on one side to create a platform for marginal plants that don't sit in deep water.

4 **Once you have** your built-up area of gravel, use washed pebbles to help hold it in place and to separate the two areas in your container.

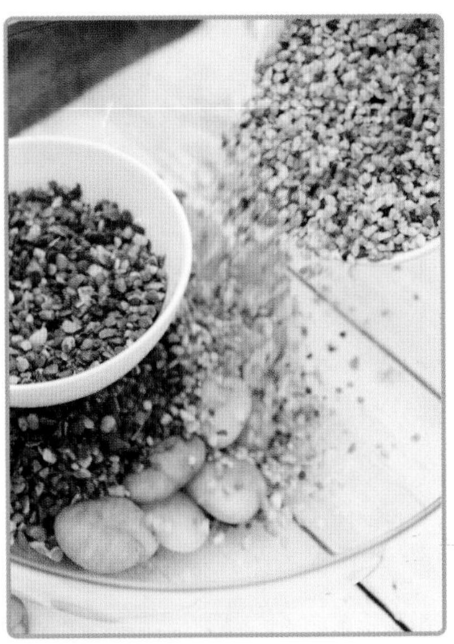

5 **Position a smaller** bowl or other container, also filled with gravel, on top of the built-up section of gravel to create the planting area for your marginal plants.

6 **Add the second**, contrasting gravel to your large bowl on the other side of the pebble divide.

7 **Plant up the** lower-level and marginal plants by simply burying their roots in the gravel.

8 **Fill the container** with rainwater or distilled water; it will look cloudy at first, but will turn clear as the particles settle. Drop the floating plants into the water and decorate with more pebbles and shells until you are happy with the finished result.

CARE ADVICE

WHERE TO SITE

Place where it will receive 4–6 hours of sunlight a day, but do not put in direct sunlight as this may turn the water green. You can keep it outside in summer but do not leave out in winter or in freezing conditions.

FEEDING AND GENERAL CARE

Use a slow-release aquatic fertilizer capsule placed directly under the plant in early spring or at planting. Liquid fertilizers tend to discolour the water. Do not feed in autumn and winter when plants are dormant. Remove any leaves or other debris, pull off any dead roots from floating water plants, and keep the water levels topped up. Try adding activated carbon granules occasionally, which remove impurities to keep the water clear and sweet smelling.

CROCHETED FLOWERS

Brighten up your home with simple crochet items. The coasters use cotton, which is lightweight and makes a good insulator. Use different-weight yarns for the garland for various sizes of flowers.

HOW TO MAKE CROCHETED FLOWERS

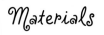

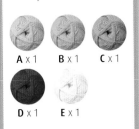

Materials

FOR THE COASTERS

Any DK weight non-mercerized cotton would be a good substitute for this project

A x 1 B x 1 C x 1

D x 1 E x 1

* 3.75mm crochet hook
* Yarn needle

TENSION
Exact tension is not essential

FOR THE FLOWER GARLAND

Any 4-ply yarn or crochet thread will substitute here or use different weight yarns for various sizes of flower

A x 1 B x 1 C x 1

* 3mm crochet hook
* Yarn needle

TENSION
Exact tension is not essential

COASTERS

(SEE P105 FOR PICTURE)

NOTE This pattern uses two shades in any combination of A, B, C, D for the main part, with the trim crocheted in E.

Pattern

With yarn A, work 4 ch, ss in first chain to form a ring.

Round 1 3 ch, 1 tr, *1 ch, 2 tr, rep from * four times, (6 tr pairs made). Fasten off A.

Round 2 Join B into any ch sp, 3 ch, 1 tr, 1 ch, 2 tr in first ch sp, *1 ch, 2 tr, 1 ch, 2 tr in next ch sp, rep from * four times join with a ss into top of 3 ch. Fasten off B. (6 tr pairs and 12-ch sp)

Round 3 Join A into any ch sp, 3 ch, 2 tr into same ch sp, *1 ch, 3 tr into next ch sp, rep from * to end, join with a ss into top of 3 ch. Fasten off A. (12 3-tr and 12-ch sp)

Round 4 Join B into any ch sp, work as for round 3. Fasten off B. (12 3-tr and 12-ch sp)

Round 5 Join E into any ch sp, 1 ch, * work 1 dc into top of each tr, 1 dc in ch sp, repeat from * to end, join with a ss into top of first ch. Fasten off yarn.

Repeat the pattern using shades C, D, and E, plus A, C, and E to make more coasters.

Finishing

Weave in all ends and press according to the ballband instructions to ensure the coaster lies flat.

1 **To join on a new** colour, insert the hook into a ch sp, wrap the yarn round the hook and pull it through to the right side of the coaster.

2 **Then make a chain** to secure the new yarn in place. Work 2 further chains to complete the first 3 ch, then continue with the pattern as usual.

3 **For the edging**, join the new colour in the same way as the other colours. Work 1 dc into each tr and ch sp around. Join with a ss.

FLOWER GARLAND

NOTE Make three of each colour in every size of flower, making nine of each in total.

Big flower (make 9)

Work 5 ch, ss in first ch to form a ring.

Round 1 1 ch, work 16 dc into ring, join round with a ss into first ch.

Round 2 4 ch, (1 dtr, 2 ch) into next st, *1 dtr into next st, (1 dtr, 2 ch) into next st; rep from * to end of round, join round with a ss into top of 4 ch.

Round 3 1 ch, (1 htr, 2 tr, 1 dtr, 2 tr, 1 htr) all into next 2-ch sp, *1 dc in between next 2 dtr, (1 htr, 2 tr, 1 dtr, 2 tr, 1 htr) all into next 2-ch sp; rep from * to end of round, join round with a ss into first ch.

Fasten off yarn, weave in ends.

Medium flower (make 9)

Work 5 ch, ss in first ch to form a ring.

Round 1 1 ch, work 12 dc into ring, join round with a ss into first ch.

Round 2 3 ch, (1 tr, 2 ch) into next st, *1 tr into next st, (1 tr, 2 ch) into next st; rep from * to end of round, join round with a ss into top of ch 3.

Round 3 1 ch, (1 htr, 3 tr, 1 htr) all into next 2-ch sp, *1 dc in between next 2 tr, (1 htr, 3 tr, 1 htr) all into next 2-ch sp; rep from * to end of round, join round with a ss into first ch.

Fasten off yarn, weave in ends.

Small flower (make 9)

Work 4 ch, ss in first ch to form a ring.

Round 1 1 ch, work 10 dc into ring, join round with a ss into first ch.

Round 2 3 ch, (1 tr, 2 ch) into next st, *1 tr into next st; (1 tr, 2 ch) into next tr; rep from * to end of round, join round with a ss into top of ch 3.

Round 3 1 ch, (1 htr, 3 tr, 1 htr) all into next 2-ch sp, *1 dc in between next 2 tr, (1 htr, 3 tr, 1 htr) all into next 2-ch sp; rep from * to end of round, join round with a ss into first ch.

Fasten off yarn, weave in ends.

Finishing

Work a chain of desired length, threading through the middle of the flowers to create a garland. Alternatively, mount individual flowers onto a safety pin or brooch back to create a corsage.

1 **Work around** the central circle to create five petals. Work a double crochet into the space between the next 2 dtr after each petal.

2 **Crochet a series** of stitches around each flower for petals. You will need double crochet, half treble, and treble stitch. Work the same number of stitches into each chain space.

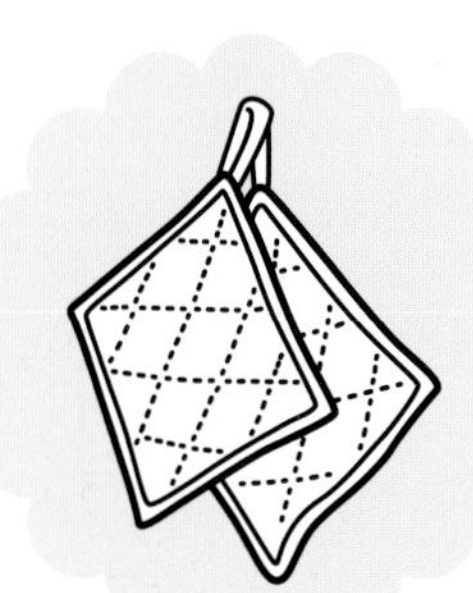

QUILTED POT HOLDER

These pot holders are quick to whip up in any size. Each pot holder is like a mini-quilt with a backing, wadding, and front all quilted together and bound. They're the perfect project for trying out your quilting skills, or using up scraps of fabric.

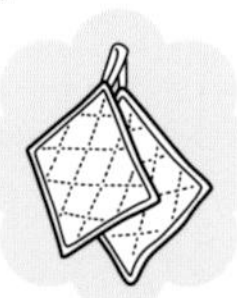

HOW TO MAKE A QUILTED POT HOLDER

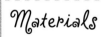

Materials

- 21.5 x 43cm (8½ x 17in) main, patterned cotton fabric
- 21.5 x 43cm (8½ x 17in) insulated wadding
- 21.5 x 43cm (8½ x 17in) cotton towelling fabric
- Quilter's ruler
- Cutting mat
- Rotary cutter
- Pins
- Sewing machine
- Threads to match the fabrics & binding tapes
- 100cm (40in) bias binding tape

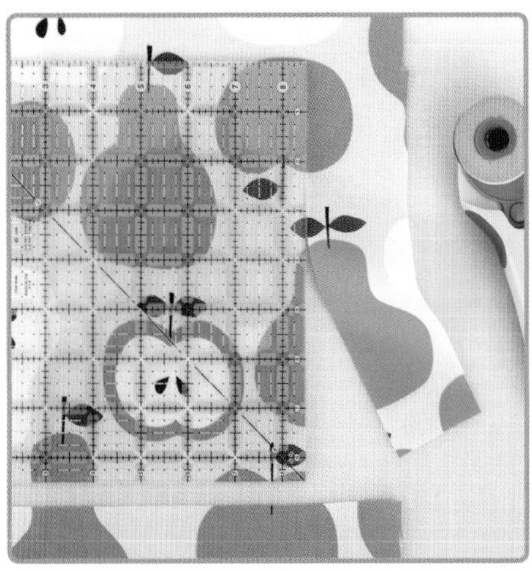

1 **Cut one piece** of main fabric, one piece of insulated wadding, and one piece of towelling fabric all 21.5cm (8½in) square. Then, cut one piece of main fabric, one piece of towelling fabric, and one piece of insulated wadding all 16.5 x 21.5cm (6½ x 8½in).

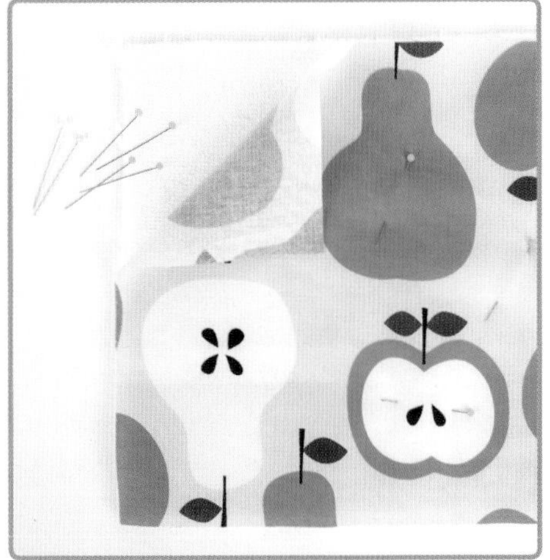

2 **Pin each piece** of main fabric wrong sides together with its corresponding piece of towelling, placing the insulated wadding in the middle. Place the pins inside the motif to be quilted so that they will not be in the way of your stitching lines.

3 **Using a matching** or complementary thread in the top of your machine and a thread to match your towelling in your bobbin, stitch around each shape on both pinned units. Alternatively, you can quilt the units using the pattern of your choice.

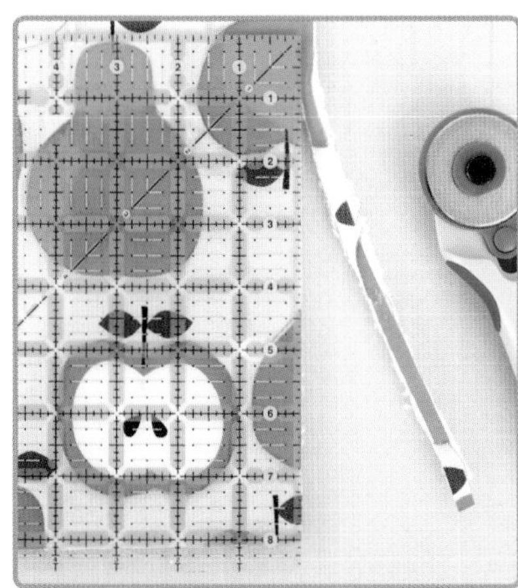

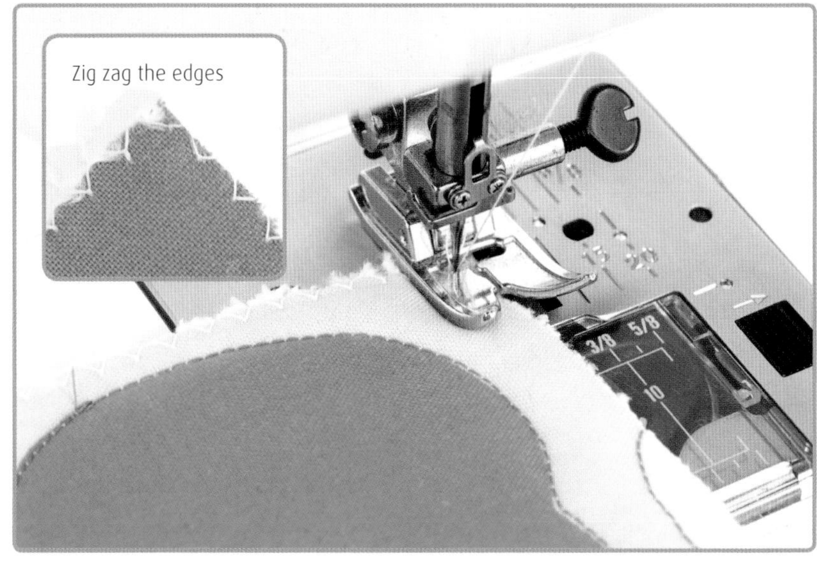

4 **Once you are done** quilting both pieces, trim the larger unit an equal amount on all four sides so that it is 19cm (7½in) square. Trim the smaller unit so that it is 19 x 14cm (7½ x 5½in).

5 **Zigzag stitch around** all four raw edges of both units to keep the edges neat and tidy.

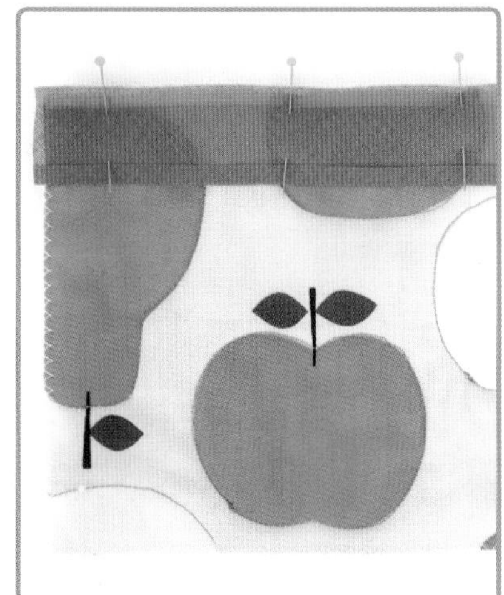

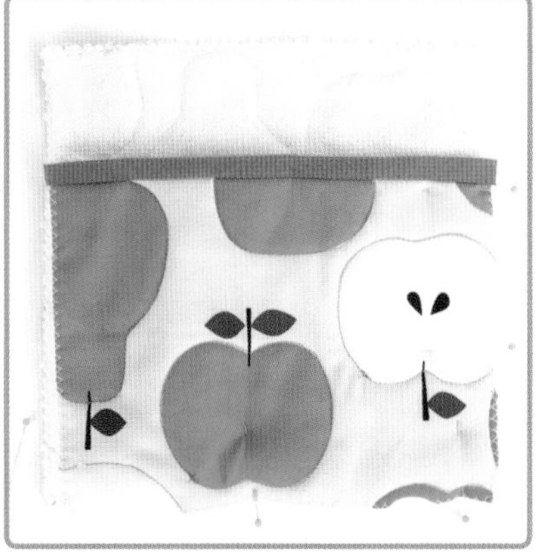

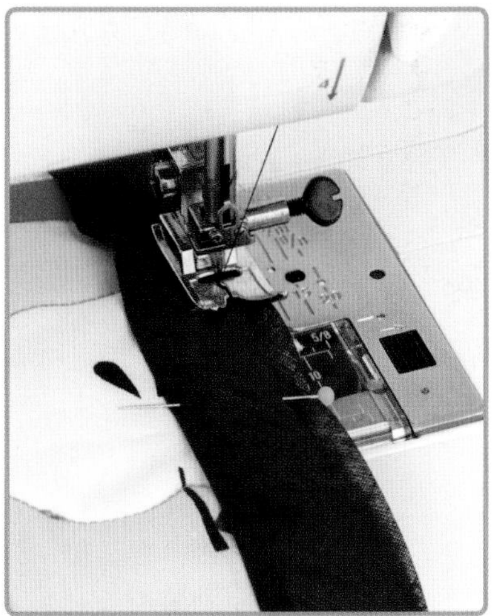

6 **Cut a piece of bias binding** 19cm (7½in) long. Open it up and pin it along the top edge of the smaller unit. Sew it in place, then fold it around to the back and stitch it in place either by machine or by hand.

7 **Lay the large unit** towelling side up, then lay the smaller unit on top of it, towelling side down. Align the bottom and side edges, pinning in place. Stitch the two units together, around the three unfinished edges of the small unit, leaving a 6mm (¼in) seam allowance to create the pot holder.

8 **Attach a piece** of bias binding to fit all the way around the pot holder, mitring the corners and finishing by hand or machine.

TWIST-TOP GIFT BOX

This ingenious gift box comes complete with its own closing mechanism – specially shaped flaps twist and lock together to hide your surprise inside.

MAKING A TWIST-TOP GIFT BOX

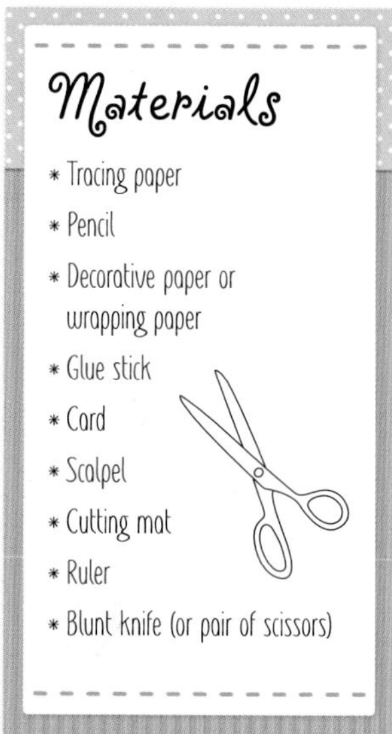

Materials

* Tracing paper
* Pencil
* Decorative paper or wrapping paper
* Glue stick
* Card
* Scalpel
* Cutting mat
* Ruler
* Blunt knife (or pair of scissors)

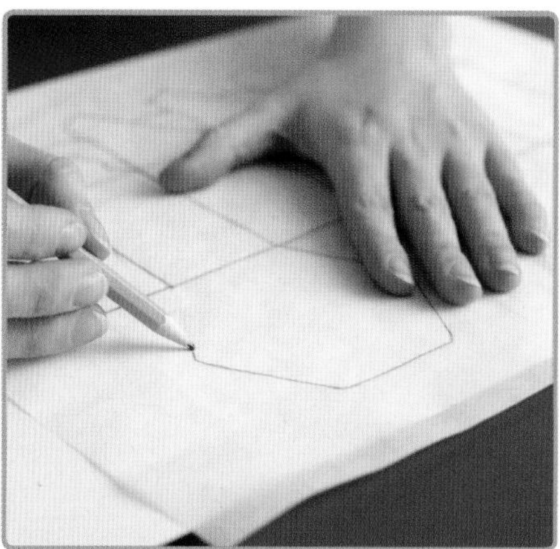

1 **Use a photocopier** to re-size the twist-top box template on pp.116–117, if required. Use tracing paper and a pencil to transfer the pattern onto a sheet of card.

2 **Glue a sheet** of wrapping paper or decorative paper to the reverse of the card. Alternatively, you could use patterned card to make the box.

3 **Using a scalpel** and cutting mat, carefully cut around the pattern. First cut along the outermost lines of the template.

4 **Next, using the template** on pp.116–117 as a guide, cut into the shape along the lines marked as cutting lines. Finally, remove the small shapes in the top as marked.

5 **Using a ruler** and a blunt knife (or one side of a pair of scissors) score all the dashed lines from the wrong side of the card. Score the lines marked with dashes and dots from the right side of the card.

6 **Fold all the scored** lines as marked, ensuring that all the creases are sharp. Assemble the body of the box by gluing both side flaps to the opposite side of the box.

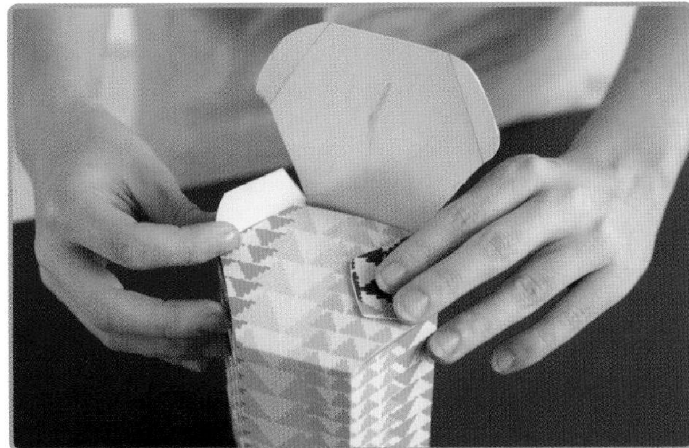

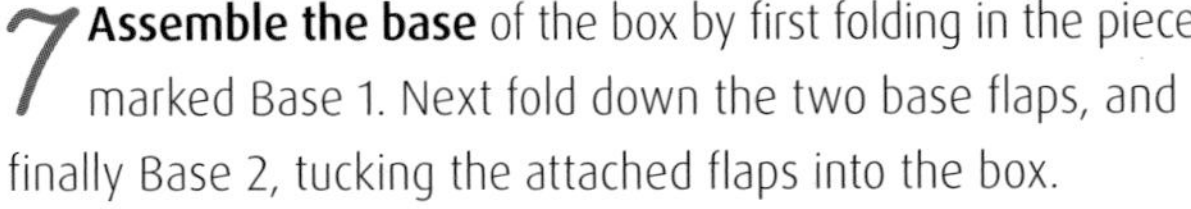

7 **Assemble the base** of the box by first folding in the piece marked Base 1. Next fold down the two base flaps, and finally Base 2, tucking the attached flaps into the box.

8 **Ensure that each** of the creases made to the top part of the box is creased in the correct direction. Fill the box and push the flaps down and towards the centre to seal it.

TEMPLATES

Template
Enlarge on a photocopier

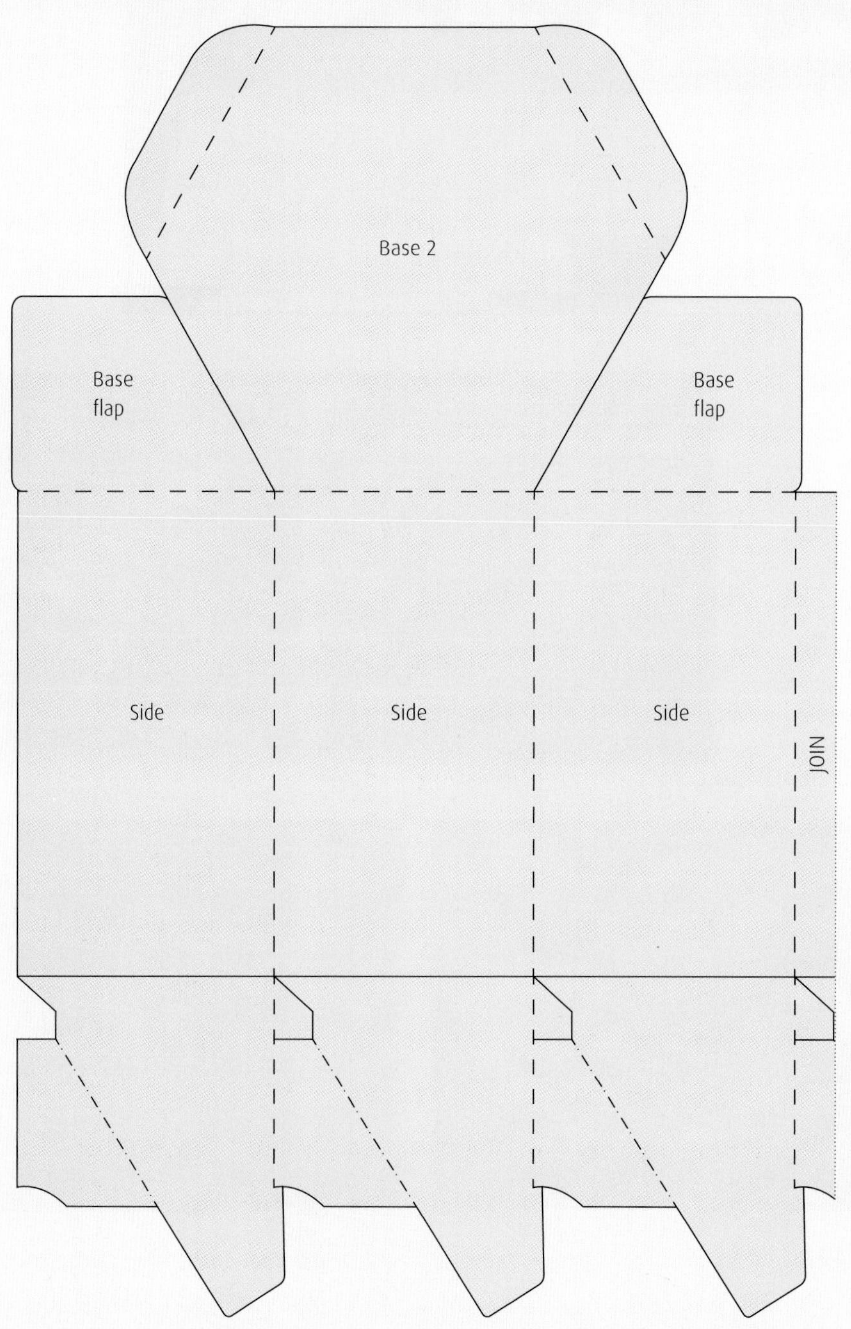

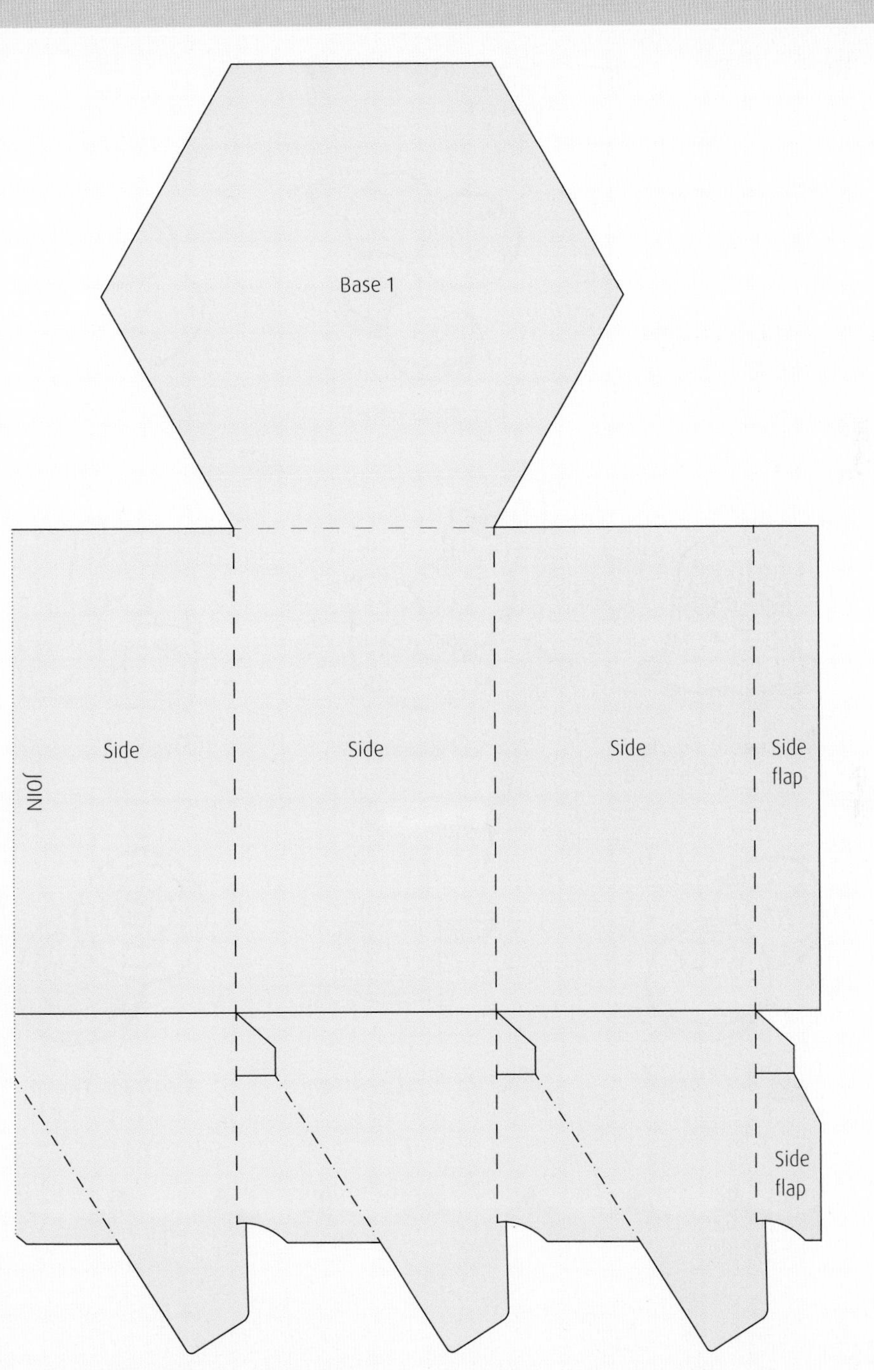
Base 1
Side
Side
Side
Side flap
JOIN
Side flap

Silhouette frame

Plum chutney

Teacup candle

Glass terrarium

Felt brooches

Fruity coasters

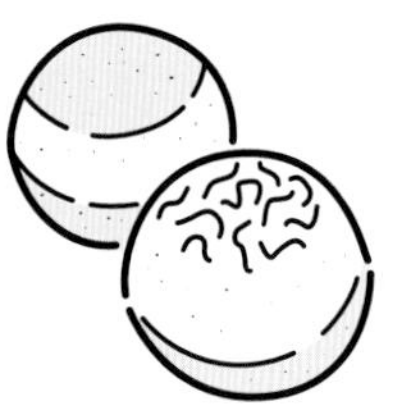

Fizzy bath bombs

Teacup bird station

Cosy knitwear

AUTUMN

Silver clay pendant

Tin can lanterns

Butter biscuits

SILHOUETTE FRAME

A modern take on the classic family portrait, a silhouette gallery is simple to put together and can make an instant impression. They're also a great way to repurpose old photos.

HOW TO MAKE A SILHOUETTE FRAME

Materials

* Photo
* Tracing paper
* Ruler
* Pen
* Glue stick
* Dark card
* Light card
* Cutting mat
* Scalpel
* Scissors
* Frame

1 **Trace around** the outline of your photo onto tracing paper.

2 **Apply glue** to the back of the tracing. Stick the tracing to a sheet of dark card.

3 **Carefully cut out** the silhouette.

4 **Peel off** the tracing paper.

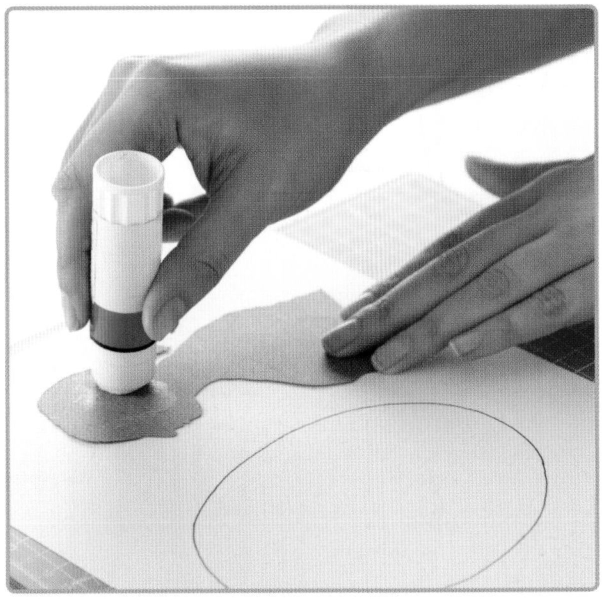

5 **Mark the outline** of your frame on a sheet of light card and apply glue to your silhouette.

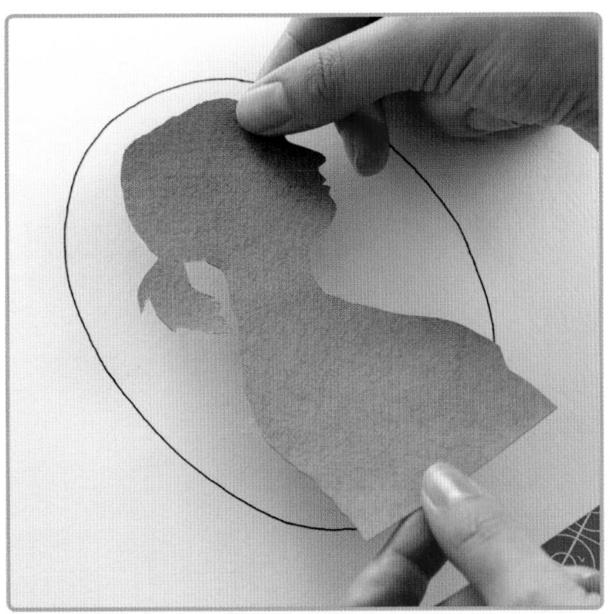

6 **Stick your silhouette** in the centre of your frame's outline.

7 **Carefully cut** around the frame's outline with a scalpel and mount it in the frame.

PLUM CHUTNEY

This basic recipe is ideal for all kinds of seasonal produce, so experiment with different fruits and vegetables – just keep the overall quantities the same.

HOW TO MAKE PLUM CHUTNEY

Ingredients

* 250g (9oz) onions
* 1kg (2¼lb) plums
* 350g (12oz) cooking apples
* 125g (4½oz) raisins
* 300g (10½oz) light brown soft sugar
* 1 tsp sea salt
* 1 tsp each allspice, cinnamon, & coriander, freshly ground if possible
* 1 dried chilli or ½ tsp dried chilli flakes
* 1 tsp fennel seeds (optional)
* 600ml (1 pint) white wine or cider vinegar

Equipment

* Sharp chopping knife
* Chopping board
* Stainless steel preserving pan or large, heavy-based, stainless steel saucepan
* Large wooden spoon
* Funnel
* Ladle
* Jars with vinegar-proof lids, or with cellophane covers and elastic bands
* Discs of waxed paper

1 **Peel and finely slice** the onions. Halve the plums, remove their stones, and cut the fruit into quarters. Core, peel, and roughly dice the cooking apples into bite-sized pieces. You can use slightly overripe or slightly imperfect produce, but carefully cut out and discard any bruised or damaged parts. The quality of the chutney depends on this kind of meticulous approach.

2 **Put all the ingredients** into a preserving pan or a large, heavy-based, stainless steel saucepan and bring slowly to the boil, stirring to dissolve the sugar. It's important to use a stainless steel pan and not a brass, copper, or iron pan, as these metals will react with the vinegar and give the finished chutney a metallic taste.

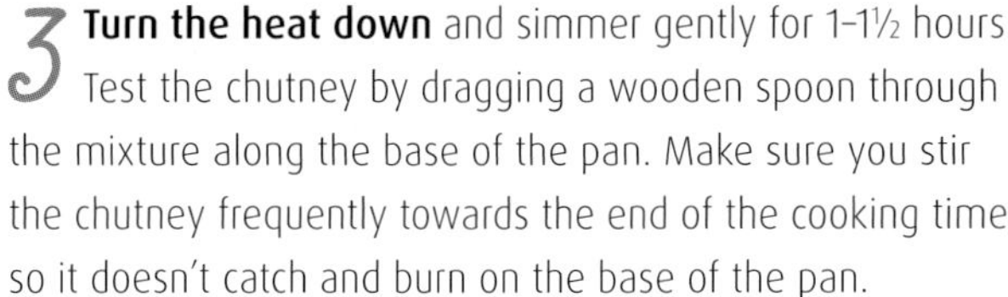

3 **Turn the heat down** and simmer gently for 1–1½ hours. Test the chutney by dragging a wooden spoon through the mixture along the base of the pan. Make sure you stir the chutney frequently towards the end of the cooking time, so it doesn't catch and burn on the base of the pan.

4 **Check the seasoning**, add a little more salt if necessary, and pot into warm sterilized jars. Cover the hot chutney with discs of waxed paper and seal the jars. Vinegar corrodes metal, so use plastic lids or metal lids that have a plastic seal or cover.

VARIATION

Runner bean and courgette chutney

Ingredients:

* 600g (1lb 5oz) runner beans, thinly sliced
* 4 courgettes, thinly sliced
* 350g (12oz) cooking apples, peeled, cored, and chopped
* 2 onions, finely chopped
* 450g (1lb) light soft brown sugar
* 1 tsp mustard powder
* 1 tsp turmeric
* 1 tsp coriander seeds
* 600ml (1 pint) cider vinegar

Put all the ingredients in a preserving pan or large, heavy-bottomed saucepan. Cook over a gentle heat, stirring until the sugar has dissolved. Bring to the boil and cook at a rolling boil for 10 minutes, stirring occasionally. Reduce the heat and simmer the mixture for about 1½ hours. Stir continuously towards the end of the cooking time to prevent the mixture from sticking and burning on the base. Test whether the chutney is ready by drawing a spoon across the base of the pan to see if it leaves a clear trail. Ladle into sterilized jars. Place a disc wax-side down over the preserve. Seal with non-metallic or vinegar-proof lids. Label and store in a cool, dark place for at least 1 month for the flavours to mature and mellow. Once opened, keep refrigerated.

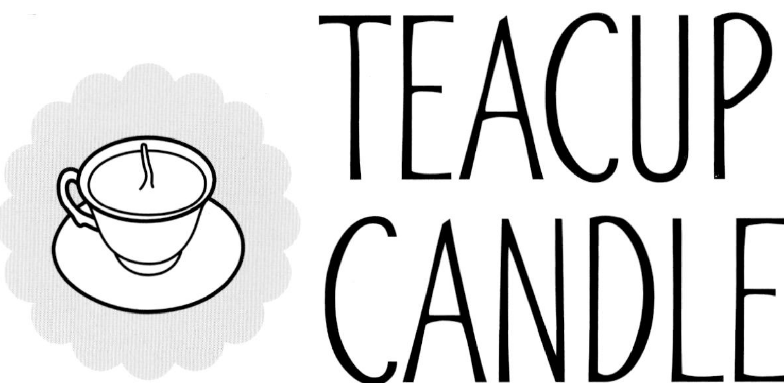

TEACUP CANDLE

This 45 minute project, is oozing with scented success – its quick, easy peasey, and fun... A good tip is to visit thrift shops regularly and build up a collection of containers.

HOW TO MAKE A TEACUP CANDLE

Materials

* Double boiler or a large saucepan & heatproof bowl
* Soy wax flakes (note the weight of wax in grams equals the volume of water the container holds in ml)
* Craft thermometer
* Heat-resistant mat or rack
* Wax dye
* Metal spoon
* Teacup & saucer
* Wick
* Wick sustainer
* 2 wooden skewers
* 2 elastic bands

1 **Boil water in the** lower pan of a double boiler and add wax flakes to the top pan. Alternatively, use a heatproof bowl over a saucepan. Heat the wax, stirring occasionally.

2 **When the wax** has melted and reached a temperature of 70°C (158°F), take the pan off the heat and add the dye – 1g (1/16oz) for each 100g (3½oz) of wax. Stir until dissolved.

3 **While the wax** is heating, prepare the wick. Attach the wick sustainer (a metal tab) to a length of wick and place in the teacup. Secure the ends of the two skewers with elastic bands and insert the wick between them. Rest the skewers on the rim of the cup and pull the wick gently to ensure it is taut and centred in the cup.

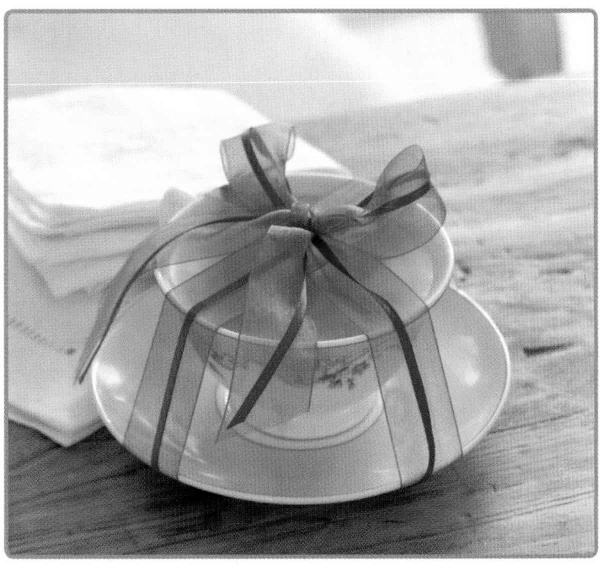

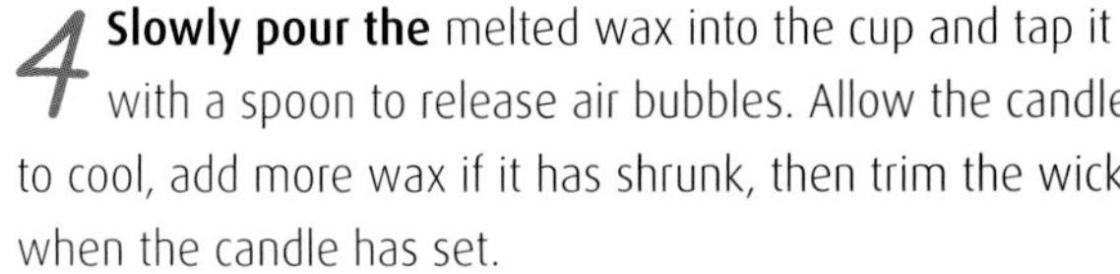

4 **Slowly pour the** melted wax into the cup and tap it with a spoon to release air bubbles. Allow the candle to cool, add more wax if it has shrunk, then trim the wick when the candle has set.

5 **If making a candle** for a special gift, tie a pretty ribbon around the cup and saucer.

SCENTED CANDLES

There are two types of fragrance oil: candle fragrance oil (a synthetic blend) and essential/aromatherapy oil (extracted from plants and flowers, and 100% natural). Both types are stirred into the hot wax just before pouring. Try different aromatherapy scents to enhance your mood or create a blend of certain oils to create an extra special scent:

* PINE OR CLOVE
To increase energy
* LAVENDER OR NEROLI
To calm, soothe, and relax
* JASMINE OR BERGAMOT
To uplift the mood and spirit
* CINNAMON OR EUCALYPTUS
To promote concentration
* SANDALWOOD OR LEMON
To relieve stress
* ROSE AND CEDARWOOD
To create a romantic floral scent
* ROSEMARY WITH PEPPERMINT
To help clear the mind
* THYME WITH GRAPEFRUIT
To create a stimulating fragrance
* TEA TREE WITH CLOVE
To create a deodorizing room spray
* BENZOIN WITH YLANG YLANG
To generate a spicy oriental scent

OTHER IDEAS

Travel candles

Handy travel candles can be made in small tins or glass jars with lids. Create them in the same way as the teacup candle (see pp.130–131). If you are using different colours or scents, you will need to divide the hot wax into batches before stirring in the dye or fragrance oil for each tin. After the candle has set, decorate or label the container as desired. These candles have each been decorated with beads threaded on a wire and a label made out of thick foil and embossed from the other side.

Layered candles

To make these layered candles, follow the instructions for making the teacup candle (see pp.130–131). Divide the melted wax into batches – one for each colour you want – and stir in the dyes. With the wick in place, pour the first layer of coloured wax into the glass, tap to release air bubbles, and allow to set. When it is solid to the touch, reheat the next batch of wax and pour in, and repeat for each layer. Leave for 24 hours until fully set.

Candles in ramekins

Ramekins – small dishes that are usually used for individual pudding portions – are ideal for making a set of candles to give as a gift. The ramekins can be washed and reused as long as the candles have been made with soy wax flakes. (Alternatively, pop them in a freezer for a few hours and the wax should drop out.) Use the method for making the teacup candle on pp.130–131.

Three-wick candle

This impressive three-wick candle can be created in the same way as the teacup candle (see pp.130–131), but you will need another set of skewers to hold the third wick (you should be able to get two wicks into the first set). Multi-wick candles give off more fragrance as well as more light.

GLASS TERRARIUM

A mini garden encased in glass, a terrarium makes an eye-catching display and is the perfect choice if you lack space. They are easy to look after, so even better if you lack green fingers.

HOW TO MAKE A GLASS TERRARIUM

Materials

* Clear glass container with lid or dome, such as a hurricane lamp, preserving jar, bell cloche, or cake cover
* Gravel or small pebbles
* Small compost scoop or spoon
* Activated carbon granules
* John Innes No. 2 potting compost
* Dibber, chopstick, or pencil
* Bonsai or ordinary tweezers
* Water mister

Plant list

* Carpet moss
* *Dionaea muscipula*
* *Hosta* 'Blue Mouse Ears'
* *Hosta* 'Cracker Crumbs'
* *Hosta* 'Iced Lemon'
* *Nepenthes x ventrata*
* *Scleranthus uniflorus*
* *Utricularia sandersonii*

1 **Choose a transparent** container and lid appropriate to the size of your plants, with room for the planting medium and growing. Terrariums have no drainage holes so, to keep roots from rotting, it is vital to include a generous layer of gravel for excess water to collect.

2 **Use a spoon** to sprinkle a thin layer of activated carbon granules (available from aquatic suppliers) over the gravel. This will help to keep the container smelling sweet by filtering out impurities. Wash the carbon granules first to remove any residue.

3 **Next, add some** planting medium. What you put in depends on the plants you choose, but a peat-like compost that retains moisture and allows drainage is a good choice. Add a layer of the compost and lightly pat down with a dibber, chopstick, or pencil.

4 **Get your plants** ready for planting by removing any loose soil and gently teasing any pot-bound roots. Make a small depression in the compost, then carefully position your plant in the soil.

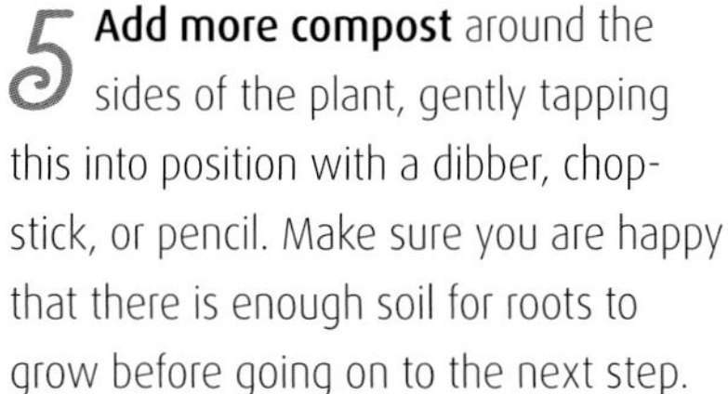

5 **Add more compost** around the sides of the plant, gently tapping this into position with a dibber, chop-stick, or pencil. Make sure you are happy that there is enough soil for roots to grow before going on to the next step.

6 **Fill in around** the plants with moss using tweezers. You can also add items from nature, such as twigs, driftwood, stones, pebbles, or shells to create a mini landscape scene in the terrarium.

7 **Remove soil from** the sides of the glass with a mister. Water then seal and leave the terrarium to create its own atmosphere. If the glass mists up inside, it is working!

CARE ADVICE

WHERE TO SITE

You must place your terrarium out of direct sunlight, so don't choose a sunny windowsill. They need low light, but enough to be able to grow without becoming straggly.

WATERING

The key to a terrarium is that it is self-sufficient. Plants form condensation in the enclosed environment, water drips down the sides and they water themselves. If the condensation stops or the soil looks dry, water plants by using a meat baster or misting the inside. Don't overwater, especially in winter. Tropical or carnivorous plants need a bit more water, preferring rainwater, and while they do not enjoy being soggy they must always be wet, so maintain the water level at 5cm (2in) below the surface of the soil. Add more sand to the planting medium for these plants, too.

GENERAL CARE

Air the terrarium every 2–3 weeks for a few hours, especially in the spring and summer.

If you've chosen the right plants and the right container size to match, the terrarium will keep going for a while, without needing replacement plants. You can keep plants in shape by pruning; make sure you remove any trimmed foliage and any plant that begins to rot. Plants rot because of too much moisture, so you will need to redress the balance by opening the lid more frequently. The soil can be refreshed after a while by scraping off the surface layer and replacing it with fresh compost.

FELT BROOCHES

It's hard to believe that scraps of fabric and felt, buttons, ribbon, and beads are all that are needed to make these whimsical brooches.

HOW TO MAKE FELT BROOCHES

Materials

* Pencil
* Double-sided bonding web
* Dressmaker's scissors
* Iron
* Patterned fabric
* 3 squares of felt in contrasting colours
* Damp cloth
* 1 skein of stranded cotton embroidery thread & needle
* Extra-heavy-weight sew-in interfacing
* Cotton sewing thread
* 35 seed beads
* 1 black bead
* 15cm (6in) narrow ribbon
* 1 small button
* Brooch pin

1 **Draw a bird's body template** onto the paper side of the bonding web. Cut out the bird and iron it, textured side down, onto the reverse of the patterned fabric. Cut out the bird.

2 **Peel off the** backing paper. Place the bird face side up on the first felt square. Cover with a damp cloth and iron for a few seconds until the bird is bonded to the felt.

3 **Using three strands** of the cotton embroidery thread, stitch around the bird shape using an overstitch.

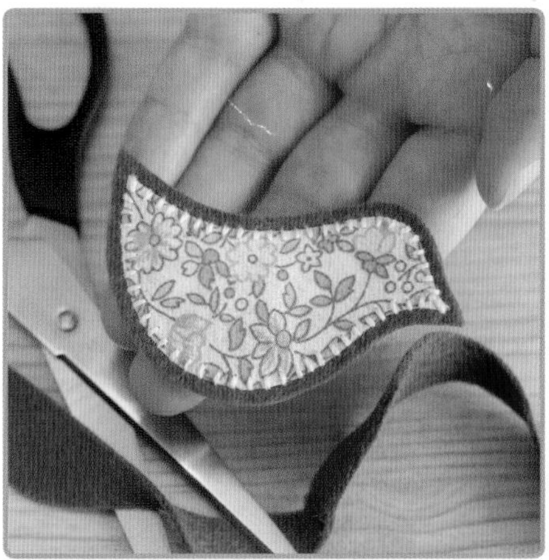

4 **Cut the felt** around the bird, leaving a felt border of approximately 3–5mm (⅛–¼in).

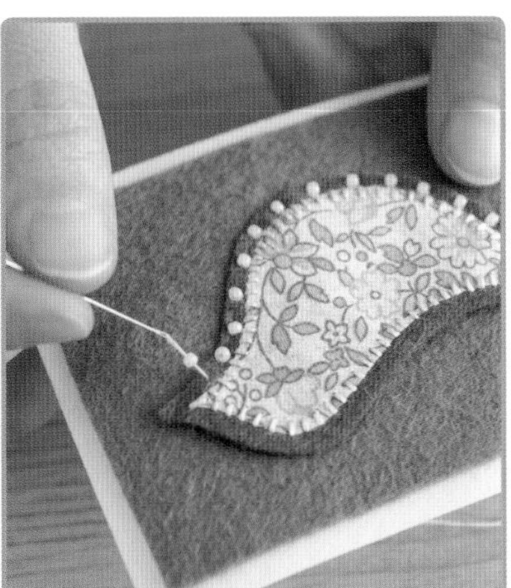

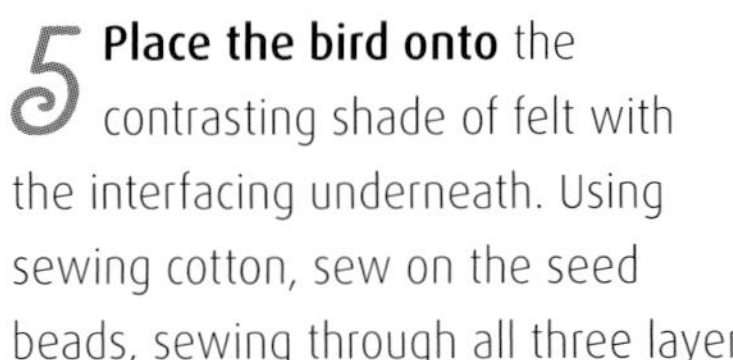

5 **Place the bird onto** the contrasting shade of felt with the interfacing underneath. Using sewing cotton, sew on the seed beads, sewing through all three layers.

6 **Carefully cut around** the bird shape, again leaving a border of approximately 3–5mm (⅛–¼in). Make sure that you cut through both the contrasting felt and the interfacing.

7 **Draw a wing template**, cut a wing out of the first colour of felt. Stitch the wing onto the bird with the embroidery thread using a small running stitch.

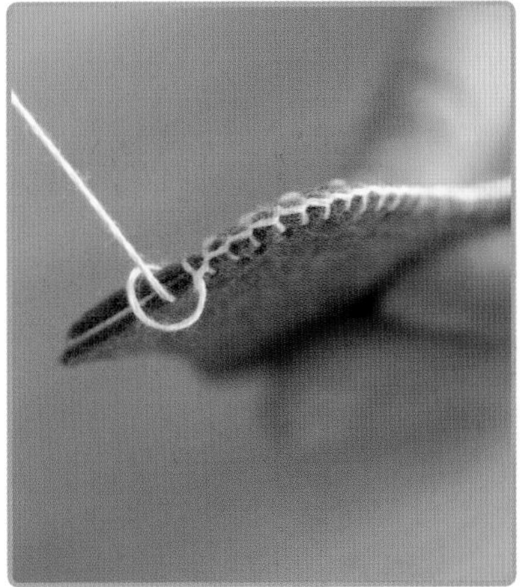

8 **Stitch on the** black bead for the eye. Cut the ribbon in half and sew on two small ribbon loops for the tail. Using the embroidery thread, sew on the button to cover the ends of the ribbon.

9 **Using the brooch** as a guide, cut an identical shape out of the last colour of felt to use as the backing. Using the embroidery thread, attach the backing with blanket stitch.

10 **Using doubled sewing thread** for strength, stitch the brooch pin on the reverse side of the brooch. Ensure you only stitch through the backing felt.

FRUITY COASTERS

Make this fun set of four fruit-themed coasters using plain white ceramic bathroom or kitchen tiles. Why not come up with your very own designs and give a set as a gift?

HOW TO MAKE A SET OF COASTERS

Materials

* 4 white ceramic tiles 10 x 10cm (4 x 4in)
* Cloth
* White spirit
* Card or thick paper
* Pencil
* Ruler
* Scalpel & scissors
* Cutting mat
* Masking tape
* Ceramic paints in turquoise, yellow, peridot green & brown
* Make-up sponge
* Medium-size flat paintbrush
* Fine paintbrush

1 **Clean the surface** of the tile using a cloth dipped in white spirit. Leave to dry. Draw templates of fruit onto card and cut out carefully using a scalpel, so that you have two stencils: a solid fruit shape and its frame.

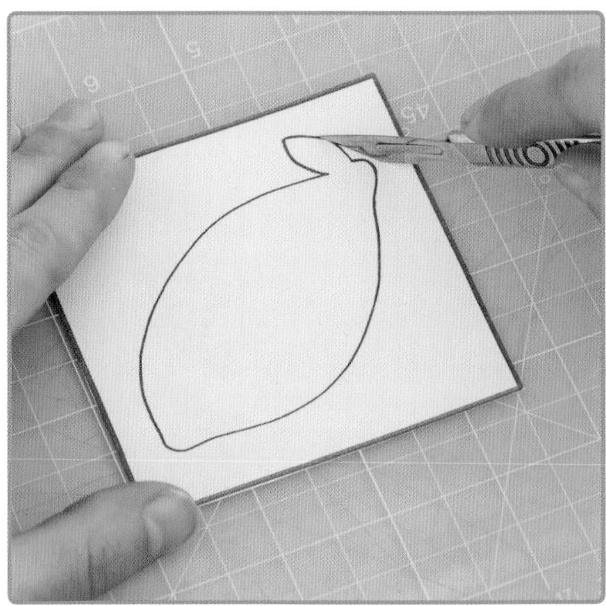

2 **Stick the solid** fruit stencil to the tile with masking tape loops stuck on the underside of the stencil. Pressing the edges of the stencil down to avoid seepage, sponge on the turquoise paint. Leave to dry for 30 minutes, then remove the stencil.

FIXING CERAMIC PAINTS

Once the paints are dry, place the ceramic tile in a cold oven and set to the recommended temperature. Bake for the stated time, turn off the oven, and leave to cool in the oven. Do not be tempted to remove the ceramic tile from the oven when it is still hot as the sudden change in temperature may make it crack.

3 **Using a medium-size** flat paintbrush, paint the body of the lemon with a generous amount of yellow paint. Leave a thin, unpainted border around the shape for effect. Rinse the brush.

4 **When the yellow paint** is dry, paint the leaf in peridot green using a fine paintbrush. Rinse and dry the brush, then paint the stalk brown: try to paint it in just one or two even strokes.

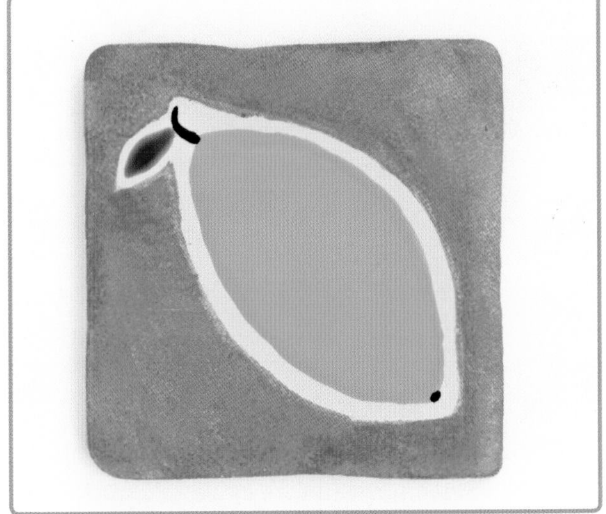

5 **Leave the tile** to dry for 24 hours. Repeat Steps 1 to 4 to apply the other designs to three more tiles so that you have a full set. Follow the paint manufacturer's instructions to set the colours.

FIZZY BATH BOMBS

Bath bombs are solid balls that fizz and bubble as they dissolve, adding scent and colour to the bath water. They make wonderful gifts and are surprisingly easy to make.

HOW TO MAKE FIZZY BATH BOMBS

Materials

* 155g (5½oz) bicarbonate of soda
* Sieve
* 1 medium mixing bowl
* 75g (2½oz) citric acid
* 2 small mixing bowls
* ¼ tsp purple natural mineral colour
* Spoon
* ½ tsp juniper essential oil
* Water in a spray bottle
* Bath bomb mould

1 **Measure out** the bicarbonate of soda and sieve it into the larger mixing bowl.

2 **Add the citric acid** to the bicarbonate of soda and mix well with your fingers until fully combined.

3 **Split the mixture** between the two smaller bowls. Add the colour to the first bowl and mix well with a spoon or your fingers, ensuring no lumps remain.

4 **Add approximately** half the fragrance to the first bowl and half to the second bowl. Mix each bowl well, again making sure that no lumps remain.

5 **Spray both bowls** lightly with water and mix it in evenly with your fingers. Continue to spritz and mix until the mixture feels damp but not too moist.

6 **Fill one of the mould** halves halfway with the purple mixture. Gently press the mixture down into the mould with your fingers to remove any pockets of air.

7 **Add white mixture** to the mould half, leaving a mound at the top. Repeat the process for the other mould half, this time starting with the white mixture.

8 **Bring the two mould** halves together, making sure that the two halves of the bath bomb are lined up exactly. Press the halves together.

9 **Leave the bath bomb** to set for approximately five minutes. Try not to move it at all during this time, as it can be very fragile before it is set.

10 **Once set**, remove one of the mould halves. Then place your palm over the bath bomb and gently turn it over. Remove the other mould half.

TEACUP BIRD STATION

Watching birds in your outdoor space is both fascinating and relaxing. Add a decorative touch while looking after your feathered friends with these delightful feeders made from cups, mugs, and bowls.

MAKING A TEACUP BIRD STATION

Materials

* Terracotta drip trays
* Bamboo canes, cut to slightly different lengths
* Acrylic or exterior paints
* Paintbrushes
* Clear yacht varnish (optional)
* Selection of large ceramic or enamel cups, mugs & small bowls
* Masking tape
* Electric drill with ceramic & metal drill bits
* Exterior glue
* Cane toppers
* Bricks or large stones (optional)
* Bird seed

1 **Paint the drip trays** and canes in a variety of colours. Think how they will work with your cups and bowls when choosing your colours, and try matching or contrasting the colours of the trays and canes. Leave to dry and then add a coat of yacht varnish, if you like, for extra protection against the elements.

2 **Drill a hole** in the base of each of your seed holders. This will help rainwater to drain away so that the bird seed doesn't get too waterlogged. Make a masking-tape cross where you want to drill for a neat finish and to prevent slipping.

3 **Glue a cane topper** onto one end of each cane and leave to dry.

4 **Apply glue to** the tops of the cane toppers, then glue these to the middle of each of the painted terracotta saucers. Leave to dry completely.

5 **Apply several dabs** of glue to the base of each cup or bowl and stick them in place on the saucers. Don't glue all the way round – this will allow water to drain out easily.

6 **Insert the canes** firmly into the ground. Support with stones if needed, then fill with beed seed.

COSY KNITWEAR

Get ready for the cold weather with this fabulous knitted scarf and snood. Embellish as you wish – buttons, rosettes, and pom poms will all look great.

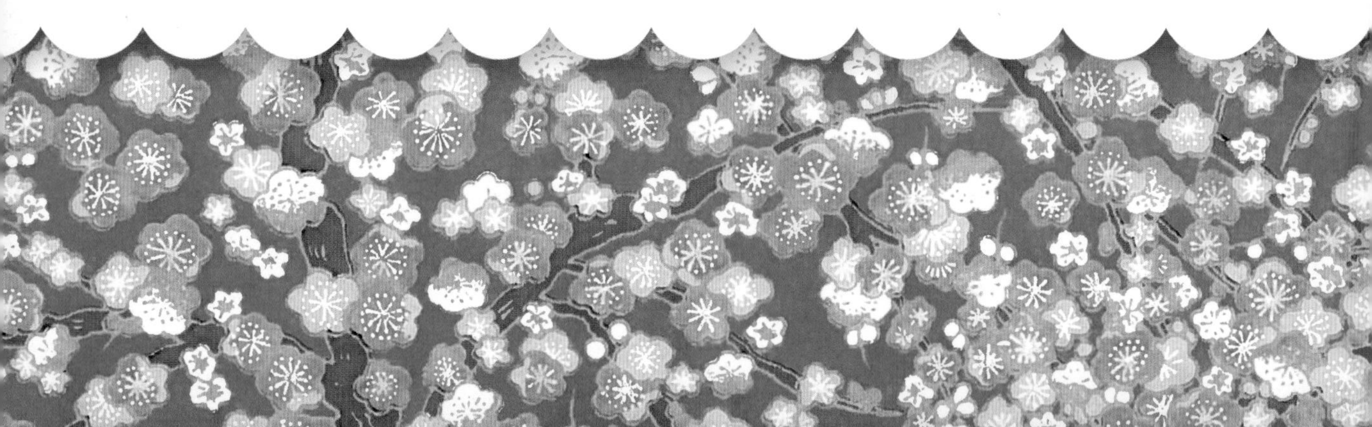

HOW TO MAKE COSY KNITWEAR

Materials

FOR THE LOOP EDGE SCARF

* Rowan Big Wool 100g 58 Heather x 3

SB heather x 3

* 1 pair of 10mm (UK000/US15) needles
* 1 spare needle or stitch holder
* Large-eyed needle

SPECIAL ABBREVIATIONS

mL Make a loop

TENSION

11sts and 20 rows to 10cm (4in) over g st on 10mm (UK000/US15) needles

LOOP EDGE SCARF

(SEE P155 FOR PICTURE)

Pattern

Cast on 14sts.

Row 1: K1, ML to last st, k1.

Row 2: P to end.

Rep rows 1 and 2 x 2, then row 1 once more.

Work g st (k every row) until work measures 75cm (30in), ending with a WS row.

Cut yarn and keep sts on a spare needle or stitch holder.

Make another section of scarf in the same way, ending with a RS row, cut yarn leaving a tail four times the width of the knitting. Graft the two pieces together. To graft garter stitch, place stitches from holder onto needle. Hold two needles parallel and pointing in the same direction, so that your knitting is end to end, and the last row of stitches facing you directly below the front needle are purl stitches and those directly below the rear needle are knit stitches. Thread long tail of yarn onto large-eyed sewing needle. Insert sewing needle purlwise into first stitch on front needle, and pull yarn through. Insert needle purlwise into first stitch on rear needle and pull yarn through.

*Insert sewing needle into first front stitch knitwise and remove stitch from knitting needle, gently pulling yarn through stitch loop. Insert sewing needle into next front stitch purlwise and pull yarn through. Insert sewing needle into first backstitch knitwise and slip stitch off needle. Pull yarn through stitch. Insert needle into next back stitch purlwise and pull yarn through.

*Repeat from * to * until no stitches remain. Sew in end. Alternatively for an easier but more noticeable join, end both pieces on a WS row. Hold both needles in your left hand, WS together and taking one loop from one needle and one from the other, cast off the loops together in twos.

Make a loop (ML)

Knit a stitch without slipping it off the LH needle. Bring yarn between needles to front of work and wrap it around your thumb from left to right. Take yarn between needles to back of work. Keeping your thumb in the loop, knit into the same stitch again this time taking it to the RH needle and letting it drop. Take the yarn over the needle from front to back and pass last 2sts on RH needle over as if casting off. Slide your thumb out of the loop.

ROSETTE SNOOD

Pattern

Using needles A and yarn A, cast on 40sts.

Row 1: K.

Row 2: K.

Row 3: *K1, p1, rep from * to end of row.

Row 4: *K1, p1, rep from * to end of row.

Rep rows 1–4 until work measures 1.4m (55in).

Cast off loosely.

Sew cast on edge to cast off edge.

Block.

Rosettes

Using needles B and yarn B, cast on 15sts.

Row 1: K.

Row 2: Kfb into every st.

Row 3: K.

Row 4: K.

Row 5: Kfb into every st.

Row 6: K.

Row 7: K.

Cast off loosely.

Roll strip into flower shape, stitching as you go. Attach button to centre of flower and sew flowers to snood.

Materials

FOR THE ROSETTE SNOOD

* Artesano Alpaca Aran 100g
* A: 2200 Laxford x 2
  B: 5083 Lomond x 1

A

B

* 1 pair of 10mm (UK000/US15) needles
* 1 pair of 7.5mm (UK1/USn/o) needles
* Large-eyed needle
* 3 x 2cm (3/4in) mother-of-pearl buttons

TENSION
10sts and 12 rows to 10cm (4in) over patt on 10mm (UK000/US15) needles

Knitted rosettes
An easy mini project, these pink roses "grow" when you knit into the front and back of each stitch to increase the fabric. They are attached to the snood with mother-of-pearl buttons.

SILVER CLAY PENDANT

Make beautiful silver jewellery items easily with silver clay. Available from craft shops, silver clay is 99% silver. When fired with a kitchen torch, the clay burns off, leaving behind a fully silver item.

MAKING A SILVER CLAY PENDANT

Materials

- Teflon mat or greaseproof paper
- Oil (cooking spray is ideal)
- Small rolling pin or piece of pipe
- Playing cards
- 7g (1/4oz) silver clay
- Real leaves or leaf skeletons
- Cutting mat or chopping board
- Craft knife
- Small straw
- Wet & dry sandpaper (600 grit) or sanding pad (220 grit)
- Firing brick or ceramic tile
- Kitchen blowtorch
- Timer
- Tweezers
- Soft wire brush
- 2 pairs of pliers
- Silver jump ring

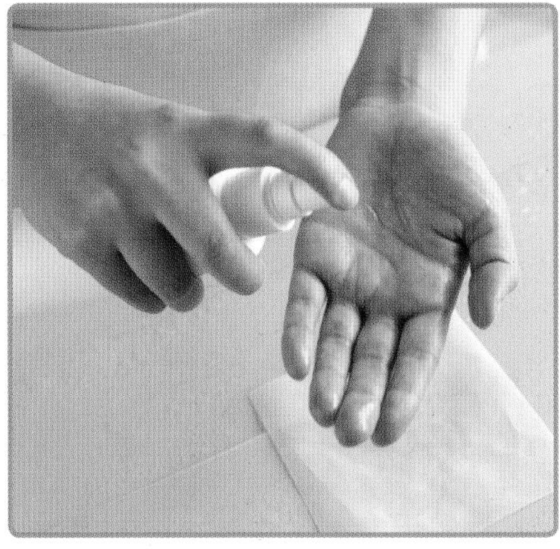

1 **Cut out a square** of greaseproof paper or use a Teflon mat. Prepare your work surface by rubbing a small amount of oil over the paper or mat, your hands, and the rolling pin.

2 **Place two stacks** of four playing cards about 5cm (2in) away from each other to act as rolling guides. Soften the clay in your hands and roll it flat.

3 **Lift up the rolled clay** carefully and place a leaf underneath and on top of it as shown, ensuring you line up the stems and tips of the leaves. Roll over the clay again to imprint both sides.

4 **Carefully remove** the leaves, and lay the clay on a cutting mat or chopping board. Using the craft knife, carefully cut a leaf shape from the clay.

5 **Using the straw**, make a hole in the leaf about 6mm (¼in) from the top. This needs to be big enough for your jump ring, bearing in mind that the clay may shrink by up to 10% when fired.

6 **Leave the clay** to dry overnight, or to speed up the process use a hairdryer or put the clay in an oven at 150°C (300°F/Gas mark 2) for 10 minutes. Once dry, sand it very carefully to smooth the edges.

7 **Place the leaf** on the firing brick or tile in a dimly lit, well-ventilated room. Hold the torch 5cm (2in) from the clay and move the flame evenly over it. The leaf will start to glow a peachy orange colour.

8 **Once the leaf** begins to glow, set the timer for two minutes. If the leaf turns bright red or shiny silver, it is too hot – move the flame away. Once fired, pick up the leaf with tweezers and quench it in water.

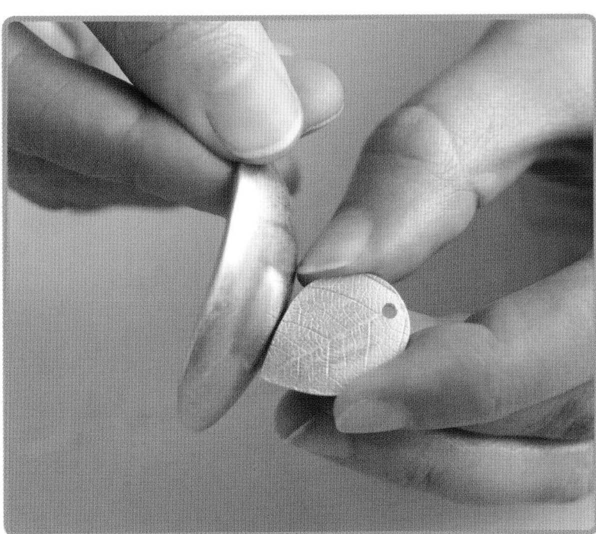

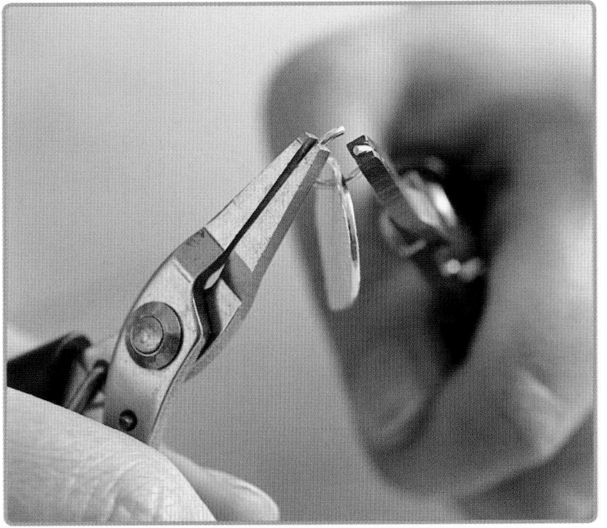

9 **The leaf will now** be a matt-white colour, even though it is pure silver. Gently brush it with a soft wire brush to reveal the silver colour. To achieve a high shine, rub with the back of a metal spoon.

10 **Using two pairs** of pliers, gently twist the ends of the jump ring away from each other. Thread it through the hole in your leaf, and then twist the jump ring closed.

OTHER IDEAS

Simple button cufflinks

A snakeskin pattern has been used to create these cufflinks made using the same technique as the silver clay pendant on pp.160–161. To make, roll out and texture approximately 20g (¾oz) of silver clay. Carefully cut out two discs measuring 2cm (¾in) in diameter, and another two of 1.5cm (⅝in) in diameter. Pierce each of these discs in the centre twice using a cocktail stick. Dry out and fire the clay. Burnish for a high shine, then with silver thread stitch the silver clay buttons onto a cufflink chain: 1.5–2cm (⅝–¾in) of chain with roughly 6mm (¼in) links is ideal.

Wallpaper earrings

Patterned wallpaper can be ideal for texturing metal clays, and the variety of designs available is huge. Make these earrings using the same technique as for the silver clay pendant on pp.160–161, using 15g (½oz) of silver clay. Using the wallpaper, roll and texture the clay as before. Cut ovals from the clay approximately 3cm (1¼in) in length, and pierce at the top with a straw. Dry out, and torch fire. Burnish for a high shine, and attach ear wires.

Leaf bracelet

This simple leaf bracelet requires approximately 25g (1oz) of silver clay. Roll and texture the clay as for the silver clay pendant on pp.160–161. Then cut out seven pointed ellipses 2.5cm (1in) in length. Pierce each end of the ellipses with a straw. While the pieces of clay are still soft lay them over a rolling pin to give them a curved shape. Leave them to dry, and then torch fire as before. Link the elements together using jump rings, and finally attach a simple clasp.

Lace heart key ring

Fabrics, in particular lace, can be used to produce beautifully delicate patterns in metal clays. To make this heart key ring in the same way as the silver clay pendant on pp.160–161, roll out approximately 10g (3⁄8oz) of silver clay. Texture it using lace, and then cut out a heart shape 3.5cm (1 3⁄8in) in length. Pierce the top of the heart with a straw. Dry out and fire the clay, then burnish to a high shine. Use a jump ring to attach the heart to a key ring and chain.

TIN CAN LANTERNS

Here's an attractive way to recycle tin cans into simple lanterns. This project uses small cans, but if you use larger ones, you might find glass jars that fit inside them to protect the candles from the wind.

HOW TO MAKE TIN CAN LANTERNS

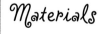

Materials

* Tin cans
* Cloth
* White spirit
* Sand
* Paper & pencil
* Sticky tape
* Fabric bag filled with sand
* Masonry nails
* Hammer
* Small mole grips
* Wire coat hangers
* Small bolt cutters
* Ring-bending pliers
* Newspaper
* Spray paint

1 **Remove the label** and any blobs of glue from the can. Pack the can with sand, top up with water, and freeze overnight.

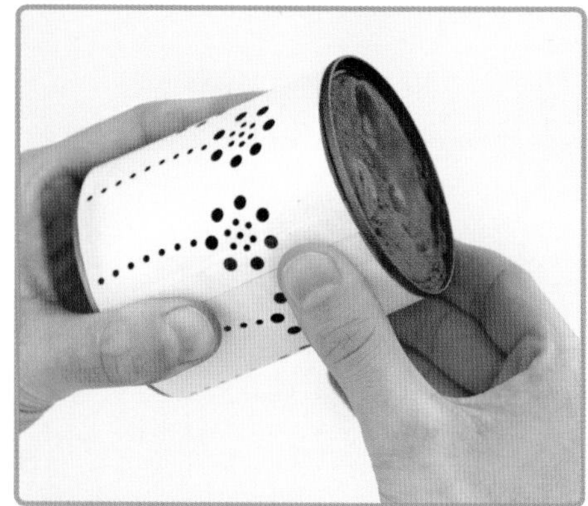

2 **Draw your design** on a piece of paper to fit the size of the can. Tape in place. If you're drawing your own design, ensure that the gap between holes is at least as large as the diameter of each hole.

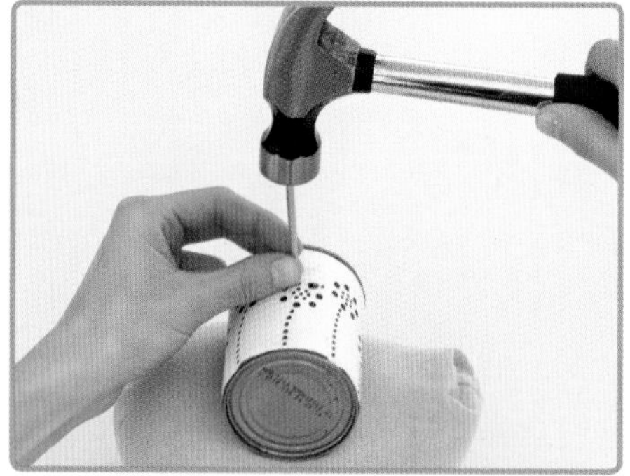

3 **Place the can** on the sandbag. Punch holes in the can. Place the can in the freezer for about 30 minutes after each 10 minutes of work to ensure the can remains solid. If you're making several lanterns, work on them in rotation.

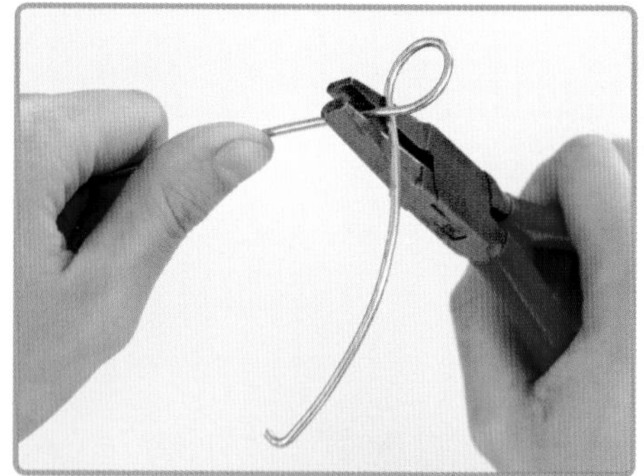

4 **Once your design** is complete, punch a pair of holes opposite each other 1cm (3/8in) below the top of the can for fitting the handle. Remove the sand. Make a handle out of a 25cm (10in) length of wire, following making wire handles on p.167.

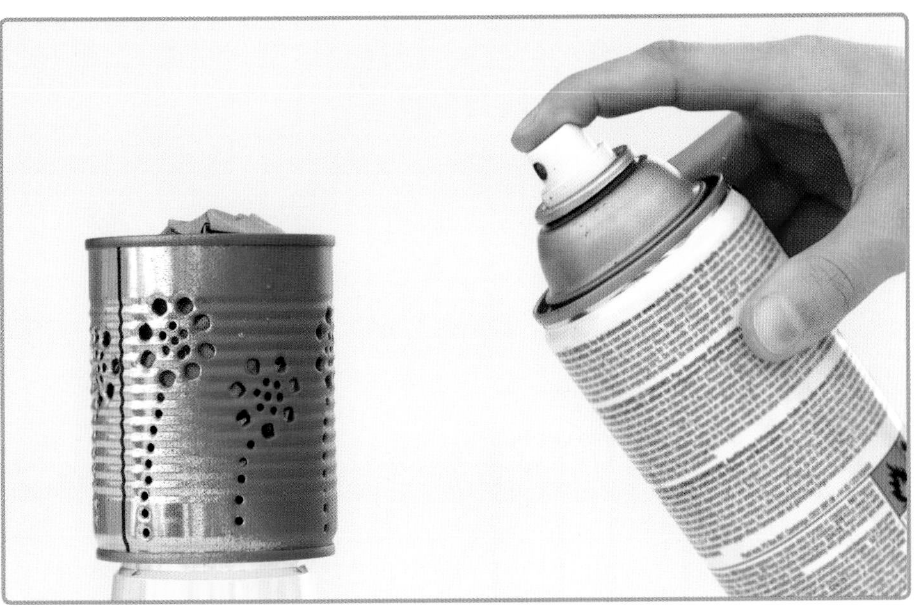

5 **Fill the can** with newspaper and spray-paint it evenly. Make sure you work in a well-ventilated area or outside. Once the can is dry, attach the handle.

TECHNIQUES

Making wire handles

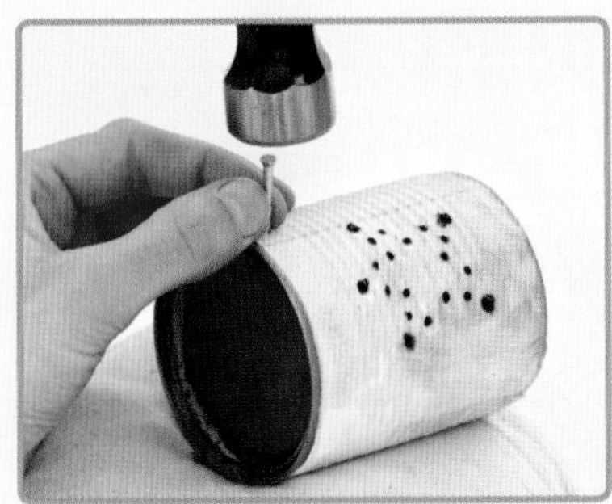

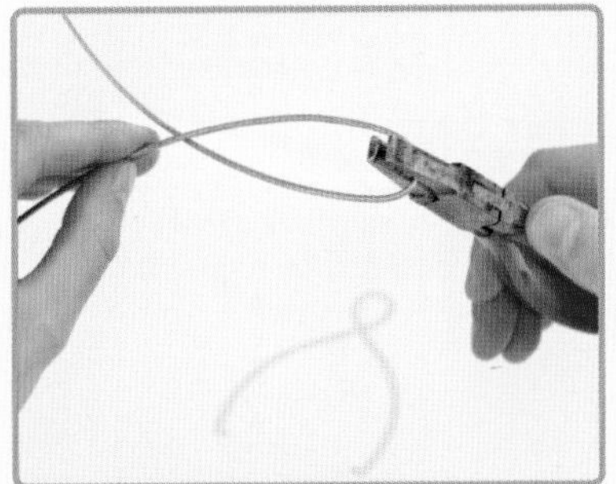

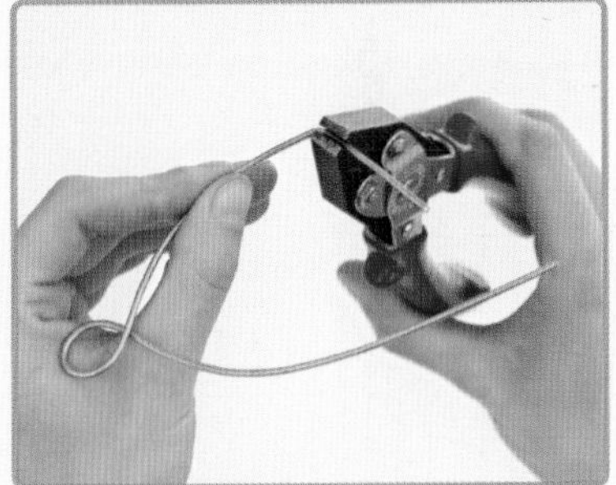

1 **To add handles**, punch a pair of holes opposite each other 1cm (3/8in) below the top of the can. Once you've emptied the can, cut a piece of coat hanger wire slightly longer than the final handle size.

2 **Use ring-bending pliers** to make a tight curve in the middle of the length of coat hanger wire. Use your hands to bend the ends into gentle downward curves.

3 **Bend the wire ends** at right angles and trim these to about 3mm (1/8in) with a small pair of bolt cutters. Squeeze the handle to compress it slightly, then fit the ends into the holes in the can – the handle should hold in place by natural spring action.

BUTTER BISCUITS

Deliciously light and crumbly butter biscuits make a lovely gift. Ensure you place them in a decorative tin or jar to make them deliciously tempting.

HOW TO MAKE BUTTER BISCUITS

Makes 30 biscuits

Ingredients

* 100g ($3^1/_2$oz) caster sugar
* 225g (8oz) plain flour, sifted, plus extra for dusting
* 155g ($5^1/_2$oz) unsalted butter, softened and diced
* 1 egg yolk
* 1 tsp vanilla extract

Equipment

* Large mixing bowl
* Wooden spoon
* Rolling pin
* Palette knife
* Clingfilm
* Round pastry cutter
* Non-stick baking sheets
* Wire cooling rack

1 **Preheat the oven** to 180°C (350°F/Gas 4). Put the sugar, flour, and butter into a large mixing bowl, or into the bowl of a food processor.

2 **Rub together**, or pulse blend, the ingredients until they look like fine breadcrumbs.

3 **Add the egg yolk** and vanilla extract, and combine together until the mixture forms a dough.

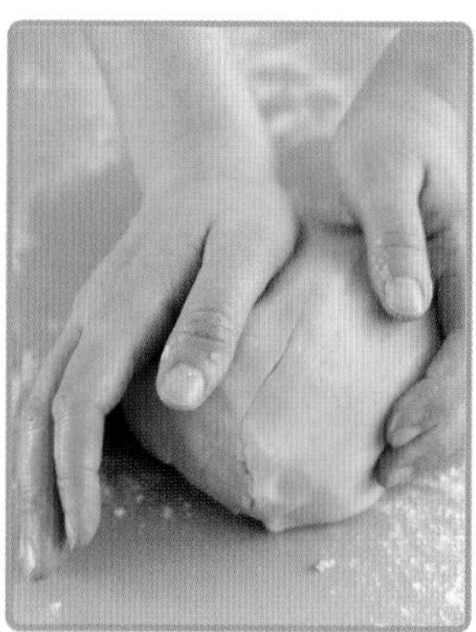

4 **Turn the dough** out onto a floured surface and knead it briefly until smooth.

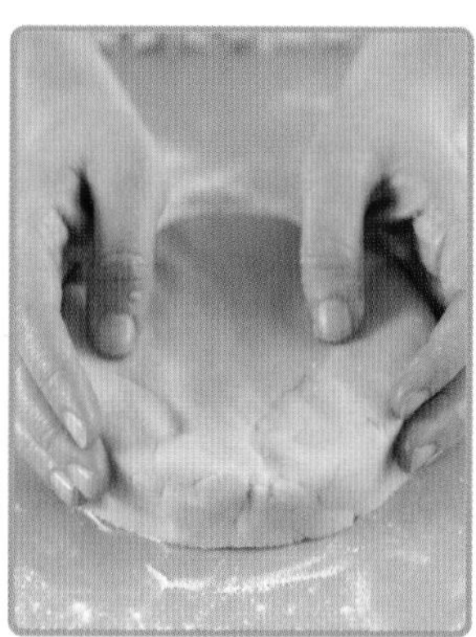

5 **Shape the dough** into a round, flat disc with your hands.

6 **Flour the dough** and the work surface, and roll the dough out to a thickness of about 5mm (¼in). If too sticky to roll, wrap the dough in clingfilm and chill for 15 minutes.

7 **With the pastry cutter**, cut out round biscuits and transfer to the baking sheets. Re-roll the offcuts and carry on cutting out biscuits until all the dough is used up.

8 **Bake in batches** for 10–15 minutes until golden brown at the edges. Remove from the oven and leave the biscuits to cool until firm enough to handle.

9 **Transfer to a wire rack** and allow to cool completely. Place in a gift box or a jar with pretty ribbons. The biscuits will keep well in an airtight container for five days.

Tartan dog jacket

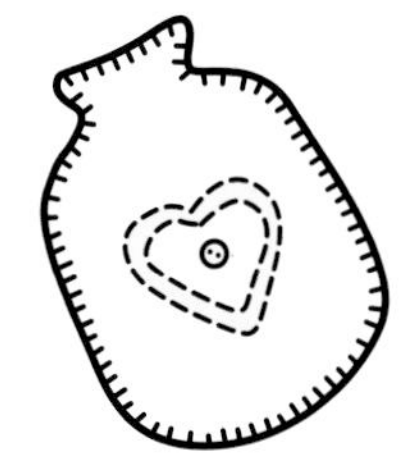

Hot water bottle cover

Chunky home knits

Mini panettone

Christmas cards

Gingerbread men

Fabric garland

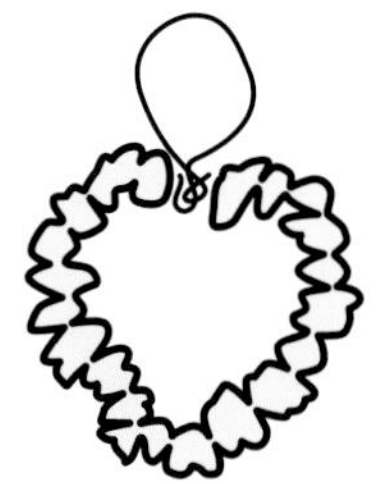

Christmas decorations

Winter wreath

WINTER

Knitted hearts

Chocolate truffles

TARTAN DOG JACKET

Keep your pooch warm and cosy all winter long with this easy-to-make, fleece-lined jacket. Adjust the pattern to fit.

MAKING A TARTAN DOG JACKET

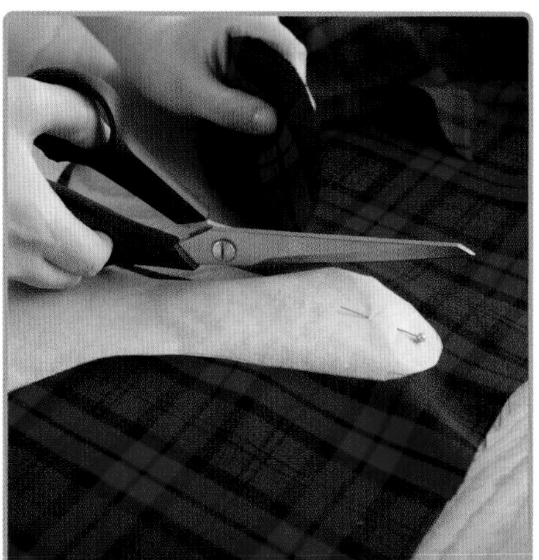

1 **Using the template** on pp.178–179, use tracing paper to make a pattern and adjust it to fit your dog. Cut out one jacket piece and one belly strap from each fabric.

2 **Place the check fabric**, right side out, on top of the wadding and interfacing. Pin all three layers together.

3 **Machine sew along** the lines of the check fabric using a long stitch, first in one direction and then the other. This quilts the jacket.

4 **Pin Velcro onto** the fleece lining and the quilted upper at the points marked on the template. Stitch the Velcro into place.

5 **Pin the quilted upper** and the fleece lining together, right sides out.

6 **Machine sew around** the edges of the jacket, joining the upper and lining pieces. Neaten the edges with a zigzag or overlock stitch.

7 **Pin the grosgrain ribbon** around the jacket as shown. Machine sew around the ribbon to attach. Fold the other half of the ribbon over the edge, and topstitch or hand stitch to attach.

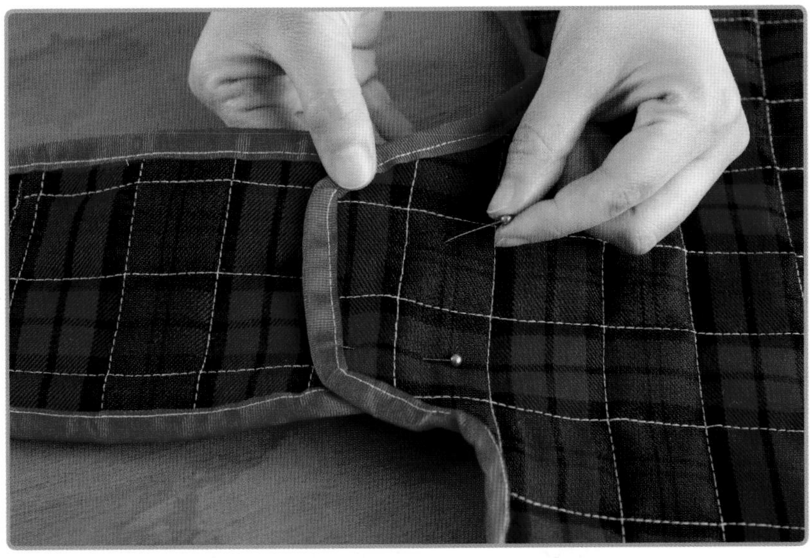

8 **Make the belly strap** in the same way as the jacket, attaching Velcro to the belly strap as indicated on the template. Pin the two sections as shown and stitch together.

TEMPLATES

Template

Please enlarge to the required size on a photocopier

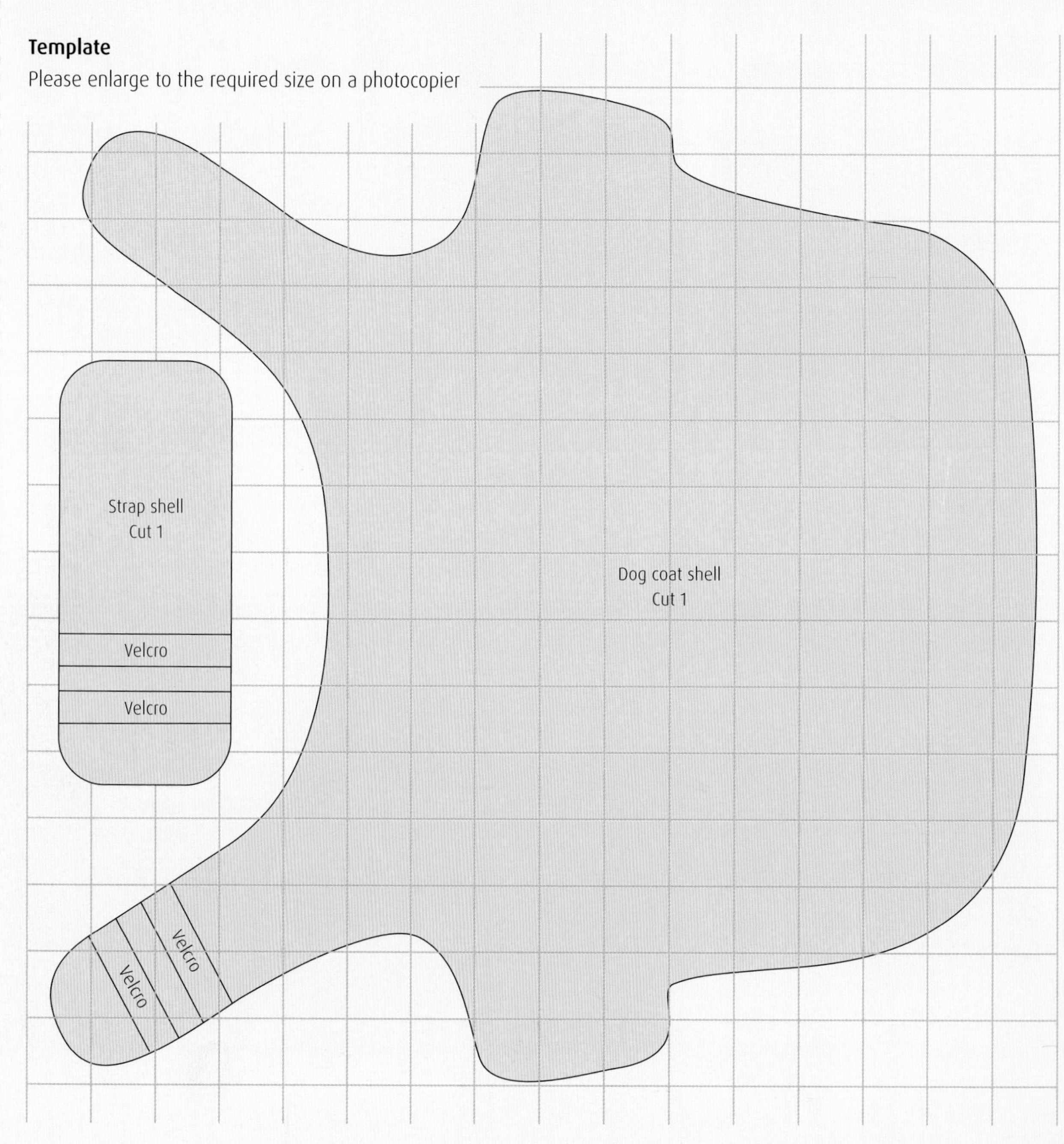

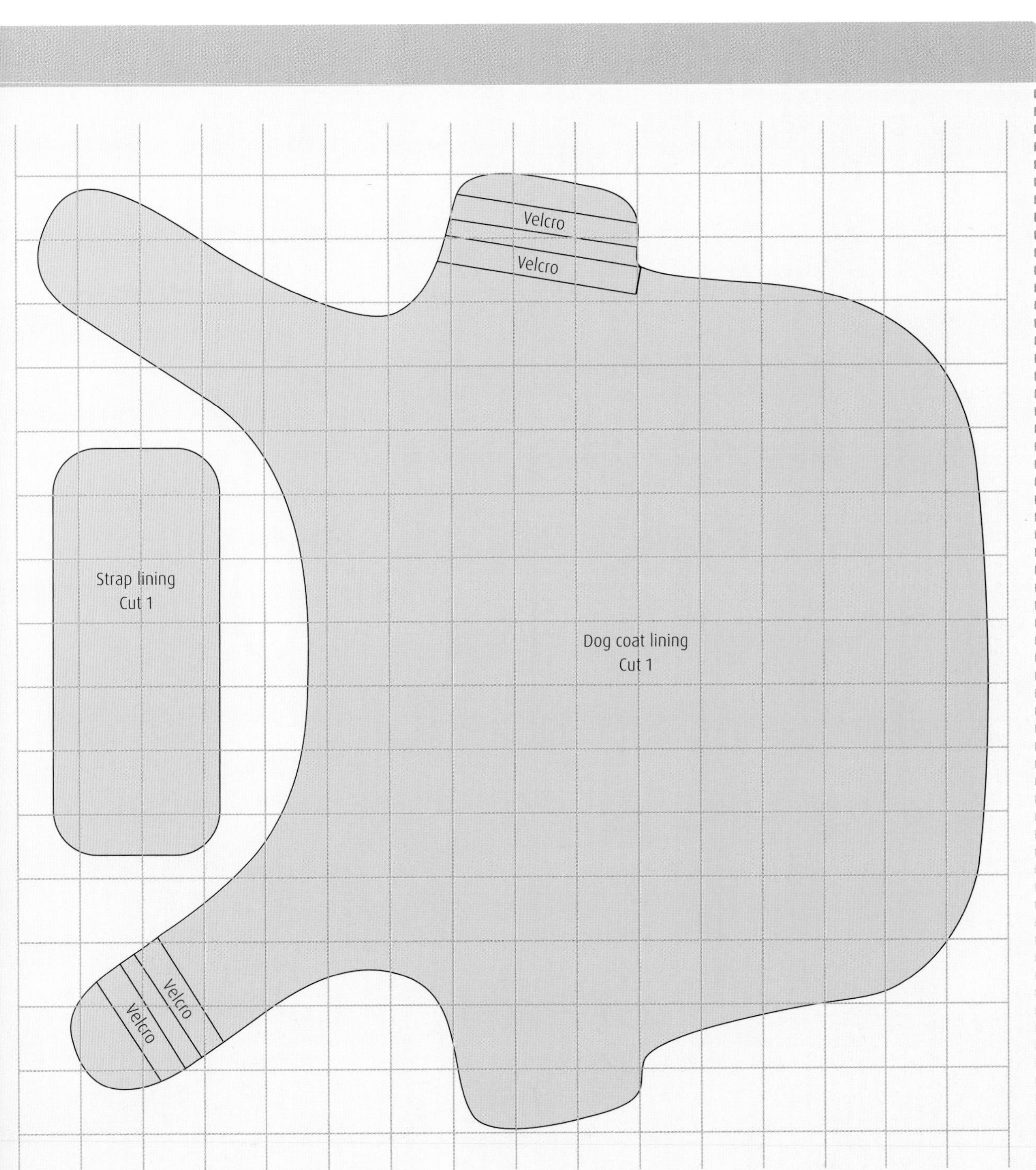
Velcro
Velcro
Strap lining
Cut 1
Dog coat lining
Cut 1
Velcro
Velcro

HOT WATER BOTTLE COVER

This lovely winter gift is quite simple to make and will delight anyone who receives it. Collect scraps of pretty cotton material, or look in secondhand and charity shops for natural fabrics with vintage patterns.

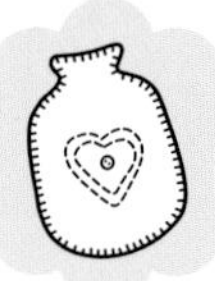

MAKING A HOT WATER BOTTLE COVER

Materials

* Woollen blanket or similar thick material
* Scissors
* 2 heart or star shapes cut from scraps of fabric to decorate the front of the cover. Alternatively, cut 2 long strips of fabric
* Pins
* Cotton thread & needle, or sewing machine
* 2 buttons
* Coloured embroidery thread & needle for blanket stitch

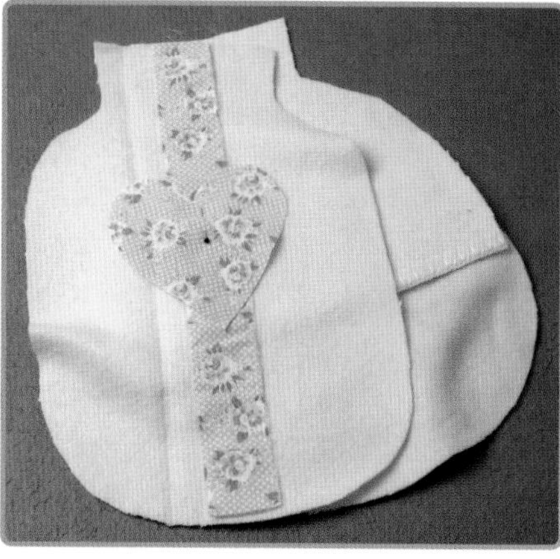

1 **Using the template**, cut a front panel and two back half-panels. Pin decorative shapes to the front of the cover.

2 **Sew the fabric shapes** onto the front panel, leaving a seam 1cm (½in) wide. Snip the fabric edges every 1cm (½in) to make a ruffle.

3 **Sew the buttons** onto the fabric shape. Sew the panels together, leaving a seam of 6mm (¼in). The back panels should overlap slightly.

4 **Using the coloured** embroidery thread and needle, sew all the way round the edges of the cover using blanket stitch.

TEMPLATES

Template
Enlarge by 225% on a photocopier

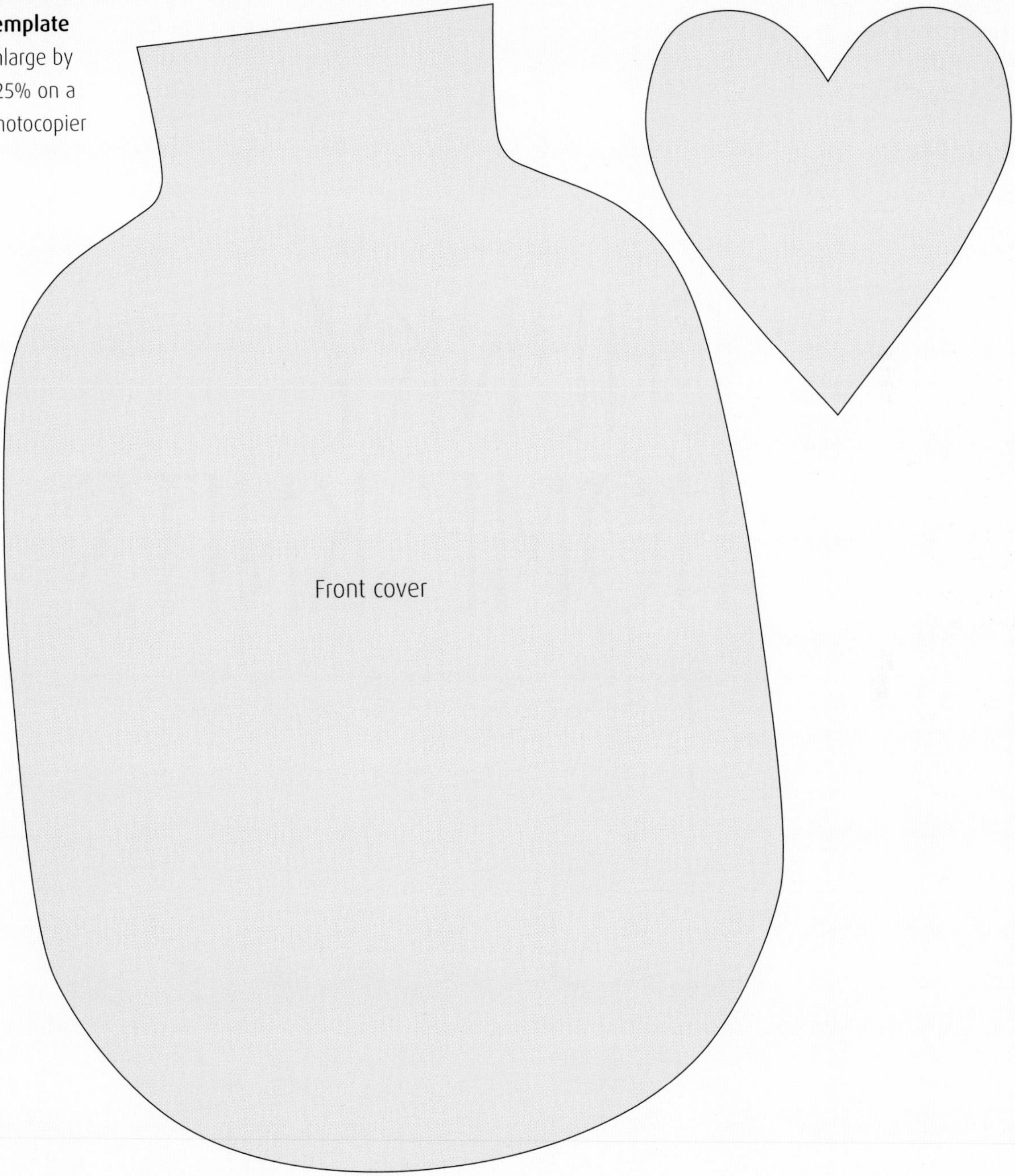

CHUNKY HOME KNITS

Snuggle up and stay warm during the winter with this colourful knitted patchwork blanket and cushion.

HOW TO MAKE CHUNKY KNITS

PATCHWORK BLANKET

(SEE P185 FOR MAIN PICTURE)

Materials

FOR THE PATCHWORK BLANKET

* Any part-balls of aran-weight or DK yarn will work for this blanket. Adjust the tension to suit your yarn specifications.

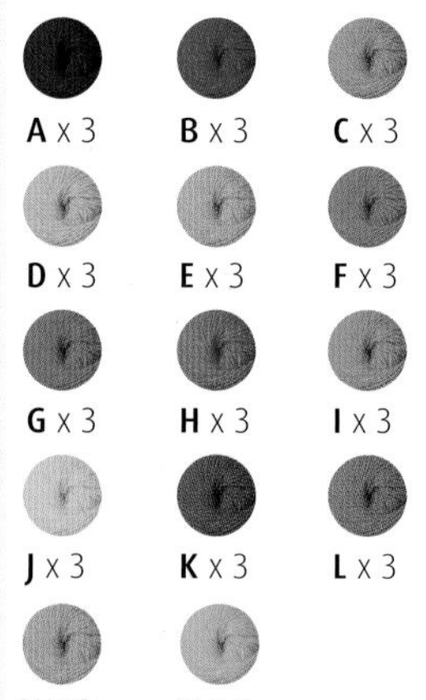

A x 3 **B** x 3 **C** x 3
D x 3 **E** x 3 **F** x 3
G x 3 **H** x 3 **I** x 3
J x 3 **K** x 3 **L** x 3
M x 3 **N** x 3

* 1 pair of 4mm (UK8/US6) needles
* 120cm long 4mm (UK8/US6) circular needle (optional, for border only)
* Large-eyed needle

TENSION
20sts and 40 rows over 10cm (4in) in g st

Pattern

The beauty of this pattern is that it allows you to use different weight yarns. However, if you find that some squares are knitting up too bulky, reduce the number of rows and stitches and/or increase the needle size for that type of yarn.

Making the squares

Using needles A, cast on 20sts.
K for 40 rows and cast off.
Rep to make desired number of squares.

Joining the squares

Using a neutral or matching colour, carefully sew the squares together using either mattress stitch or by oversewing along the side edges of the squares. Oversew along the tops and bottoms of the squares.

Adding the edge

If you'd like a border to bring the whole blanket together, then using needle B, pick up and k 20sts across each square along one side.
Next row: K1fb, k to end.
Rep last row until the border is the required length.
The blanket shown on page 185 has four rows.
Cast off.
Rep for each side of the blanket.
Oversew the mitred corners together.

Making up

Sew in all yarn ends with a large-eyed needle. If desired, block the blanket, according to the ballband instructions, and be careful not to flatten the stitches.

Square by square This simple project is a great stash buster and one to turn to between more demanding knits.

STRIPED CUSHION

Pattern

Using yarn A, cast on 65sts.

Row 1: K.

Rows 2 and 3: K.

Row 4: P.

Row 5: Change to yarn B. K2, slip next stitch purlwise,*k5, s1*. Rep from * to 2sts before end, k2 at end of row.

Row 6: P, slipping each stitch which is still in yarn A.

Rows 7–9: Work 3 rows in st st starting and ending with a k row.

Rows 10 and 11: K.

Row 12: P.

Row 13: Change to yarn A. K5, slip next stitch purlwise,*k5, s1*. Rep from * to 5sts from end, k5 at end of row.

Row 14: P, slipping each stitch which is still in yarn B.

Rows 15–17: Work 3 rows in st st starting and ending with a k row.

Rows 18 and 19: K.

Row 20: P.

Row 21: Change to yarn C. K2, slip next stitch purlwise, *k5, s1*. Rep from * to 2sts before end, k2 at end of row.

Row 22: P, slipping each stitch that is still in yarn A.

Rows 23–25: Work 3 rows in st st starting and ending with a k row.

Rows 26 and 27: K.

Row 28: P.

Row 29: Change to yarn A. K5, slip next stitch purlwise, *k5, s1*. Rep from * to 5sts before end, k5 to end of row.

Row 30: P, slipping each stitch which is still in yarn C.

Rows 31–33: Starting with a k row, work 3 rows in st st.

Rep rows 2–33 x 2. (97 rows of patt)

Row 98: P.

Cast off. Repeat for the front panel.

Making up

Lay both pieces flat, RS facing with cast off edges together (if the cast on is neater, then use those edges instead), and pin the zip centrally between the edges. Using a sharp sewing needle and sewing thread that matches yarn A, sew the zip neatly in place close to the cast on/off edge. Sew together any of the seam that is still open at each end of the zip. Turn the cushion inside out and, carefully matching the stripes, backstitch all remaining seams.

Tassels

Cut a 9cm (3½in) square of card and wind a long length of yarn A forty times around the card. Take a 20cm (8in) length of yarn A, thread it through the wound yarn at one end of the card and tie a tight knot leaving the ends free. Cut through the wound yarn at the opposite end from the knot, and slide the card out without disturbing the folded threads. Take another 20cm (8in) length of yarn A and knot it tightly around the tassel, 2cm (¾in) below the first knot. Thread the ends onto a large-eyed needle and sew them through the tassel to secure. Trim the ends of the tassel to about 8cm (3in) long.

Materials

FOR THE STRIPED CUSHION

* Sirdar Simply Recycled Aran 50g

A

B

C

* 1 pair of 5mm (UK6/US8) needles
* 35cm (14in) cream zip
* Sewing needle
* Sewing thread (to match yarn A)
* Large-eyed needle
* 40cm (16in) square cushion pad

TENSION
18sts and 25 rows to 10cm (4in) over patt on 5mm (UK6/US8)

MINI PANETTONE

A sweet bread eaten all over Italy at Christmas. Making one is not as hard as it seems and the results are delicious.

HOW TO MAKE MINI PANETTONE

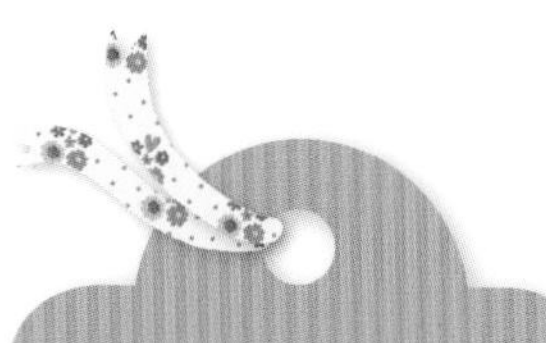

Makes 12 mini loaves

Ingredients

* 1 tsp dried yeast
* 120ml (4fl oz) lukewarm milk
* 75g (3oz) caster sugar
* 500g (18oz) strong white bread flour, plus extra for dusting
* Large pinch of salt
* 150g (5oz) unsalted butter, melted
* 2 large eggs, plus 2 egg yolks
* 115g (4oz) mixed dried fruit (apricots, cranberries, sultanas, mixed peel)
* 75g (3oz) raisins
* Vegetable oil, for greasing
* Icing sugar, for dusting

Equipment

* 12 mini pudding moulds, greased

1 **Sift the flour** into a bowl and add the salt. Whisk the yeast, milk, and eggs together. Mix into the flour.

2 **Mix together the egg yolks**, butter, and sugar.

3 **Add the butter mixture** to the batter to form a soft dough; it will be stickier than bread dough.

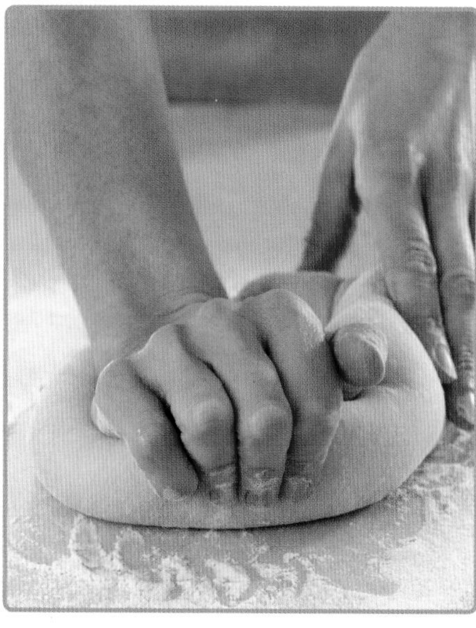

4 **On a lightly floured** surface, knead the dough for about 10 minutes until elastic.

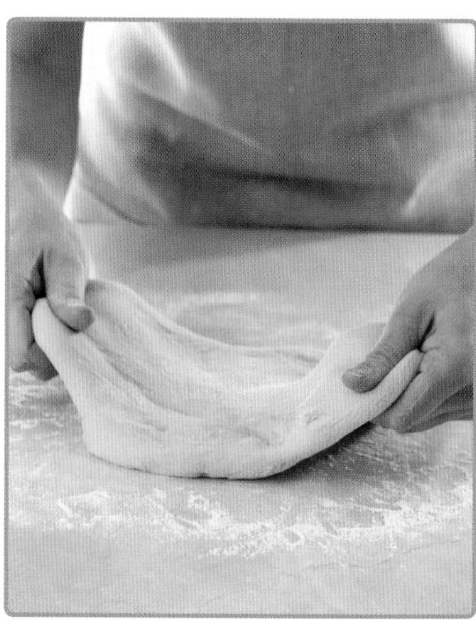

5 **Form the dough** into a loose ball and stretch it out flat onto a floured work surface.

6 **Scatter the dried fruit** on top and knead again until well combined.

7 **Form the dough** into a loose ball and put it in a lightly oiled bowl. Cover the bowl with a damp, clean tea towel or place inside a large plastic bag. Leave the dough to prove in a warm place for up to 2 hours until doubled in size.

8 **Line the tins** with a double layer of baking parchment or a single layer of silicone paper. If using a cake tin, form a collar with the paper, 5–10cm (2–4in) higher than the tin.

9 **Knock the air** out of the dough with your fist and turn out onto a lightly floured surface. Divide into 12. Knead the dough into a round ball just big enough to fit into the tin.

10 **Put into the tins**, cover, and leave to rest for another hour. Brush the tops of the dough with melted butter. Preheat oven to 180°C (350°F/Gas mark 4).

11 **Bake in the middle** of the oven for 20 minutes. If they are browning fast, cover with foil. Leave to cool for 5 minutes, then turn out; the bottom will sound hollow when ready. Remove the parchment and cool completely on a wire rack before dusting with icing sugar to serve.

CHRISTMAS CARDS

These cards are easy to make, and are a fun, child-friendly project. Tear out pages from old magazines with interesting patterns, illustrations, and festive photographs.

HOW TO MAKE CHRISTMAS CARDS

Materials

* Tracing paper
* Pencil
* Scissors
* Recycled pictures
* Scalpel
* Ruler
* Plain, recycled cardstock (or find ready-made, plain recycled cards)
* Adhesive glue

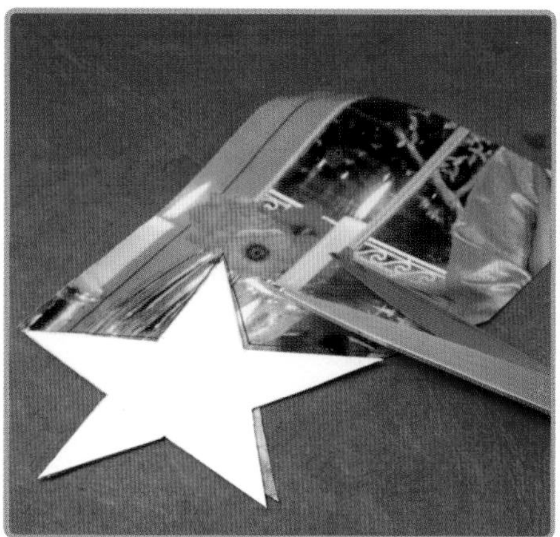

1 **Trace and cut out** the templates opposite. If you are using a star template, make up the smallest star template as well.

2 **Place the template** on a piece of illustrated or patterned recycled paper. Draw around the template and cut out the shape.

3 **Lightly score down** the middle of the recycled cardstock with a scalpel and ruler. Fold the card in half and glue the star shape onto the front.

4 **Using the smallest** star template, cut tiny stars from the recycled paper and glue them onto the card around the main star. Allow to dry.

TEMPLATES

Enlarge by 200% on a photocopier

GIFT TAG IDEAS

Dried leaf star label Glue a dried, flattened leaf onto recycled card, cut a star shape, and glue a nut in the centre.

Fabric star label Glue some cheery fabric onto recycled card, cut into a star shape, and glue on a dried bay leaf and old button.

Mini star gift tag Cut out a fabric star, glue it onto folded card, and decorate with a button and a little raffia loop.

Rustic bead label Push both ends of a length of garden string through a hole, thread beads onto each end, and tie in a knot.

Skeleton leaf label Thread a piece of string through the hole of a label and glue a couple of dried, flattened leaves over the hole.

Paper dove label Cut a dove template from recycled card, glue on festive-looking recycled paper, and cut it out.

Paper holly leaf label Cut a holly leaf shape out of recycled paper, glue onto recycled card, and add a button.

Fresh holly leaf label Sew a holly leaf onto a luggage label with festive-coloured embroidery thread using simple running stitch.

GINGERBREAD MEN

All children love to make and decorate gingerbread men. This recipe is quick and the dough is easy for little bakers to handle.

HOW TO MAKE GINGERBREAD MEN

Ingredients

* 4 tbsp golden syrup
* 300g (10½oz) plain flour, plus extra for dusting
* 1 tsp bicarbonate of soda
* 1½ tsp ground ginger
* 1½ tsp mixed spice
* 100g (3½oz) unsalted butter, softened and diced
* 155g (5½oz) soft dark brown sugar
* 1 egg
* Raisins, to decorate
* Icing sugar, sifted (optional)

Equipment

* Pan
* Mixing bowls
* Wooden spoon
* Non-stick baking sheets
* 11cm (4½in) gingerbread man cutter
* Wire rack
* Piping bag with thin nozzle (optional)

1 **Preheat the oven** to 190°C (375°F/Gas mark 5). Heat the golden syrup until it liquefies, then cool.

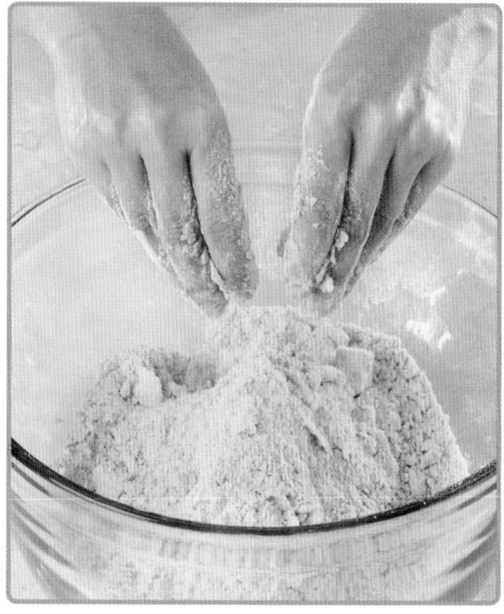

2 **Sift the flour**, bicarbonate of soda, and spices into a bowl. Add the butter. Rub together with your fingertips until the mixture looks like fine breadcrumbs.

3 **Add the sugar** to the breadcrumbs mixture and mix well.

4 **Beat the egg** into the cooled syrup until well blended.

5 **Pour the syrup** into the flour mix. Bring together to a rough dough.

6 **On a lightly** floured work surface, knead the dough briefly until smooth.

7 **Flour the dough** and the work surface well, and roll the dough out to 6mm (¼in) thick. Using the cutter, cut out as many shapes as possible. Transfer to non-stick baking sheets.

8 **Mix the offcuts** of dough, re-roll, and cut out more shapes until all the dough is used. Decorate the men with raisins, giving them eyes, a nose, and buttons down the front.

9 **Bake for 10–12** minutes until golden. Transfer to a wire rack to cool completely.

10 **If using**, mix a little icing sugar in a bowl with enough water to form a thin icing. Transfer the icing into the piping bag; placing the bag into a jug first will help.

11 **Decorate the men** with the piped icing to resemble clothes, hair, or whatever you prefer. Leave the icing to set completely before serving or storing.

FABRIC GARLAND

This charming garland is versatile enough to decorate mantlepieces, kitchen dressers, Christmas trees, and bedrooms. Store it carefully and it can be reused every year.

MAKE A CHRISTMAS GARLAND

Materials

* Large piece of cream-coloured felt
* Brown felt for the gingerbread men
* Scissors
* Pins
* Marker pen
* Coloured embroidery thread (for blanket stitching & features) & needle
* Ricrac trimming
* 5 lengths of wire, each about 8cm (3in) long
* 1m (3ft) twine or string
* Pieces of recycled ribbon
* Old, unwanted woollen garment or scarf
* Buttons

1 **Cut and pin** together two of each shape from cream felt, and two gingerbread men from brown felt. Decorate one stocking with the pen.

2 **Sew the shapes** together. Leave the mitten and stocking tops unsewn. Sew on the features and ricrac trimming.

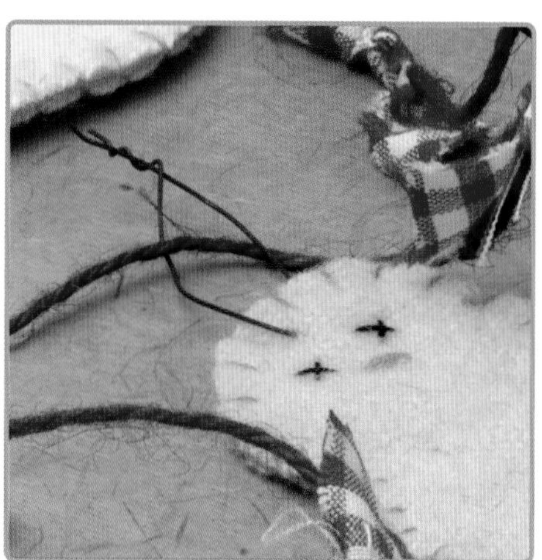

3 **Thread a piece** of wire through the top of each shape and secure in a loop. Thread the twine through the loops and tie ribbons onto the twine.

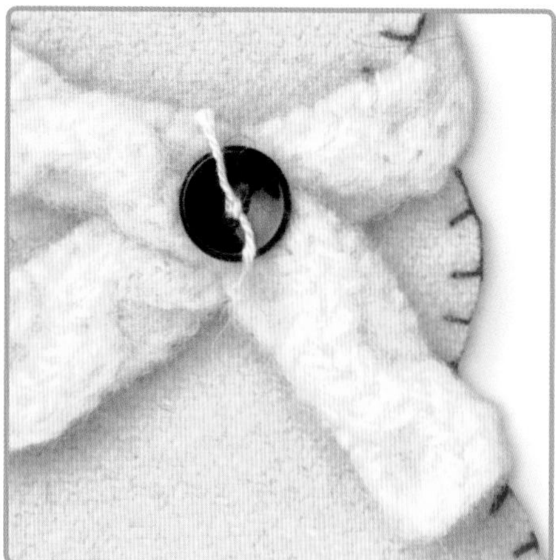

4 **Cut strips from** the garment for scarves and sew them, together with some decorative ribbons and buttons, onto the fabric shapes.

TEMPLATES

Enlarge by 200% on a photocopier

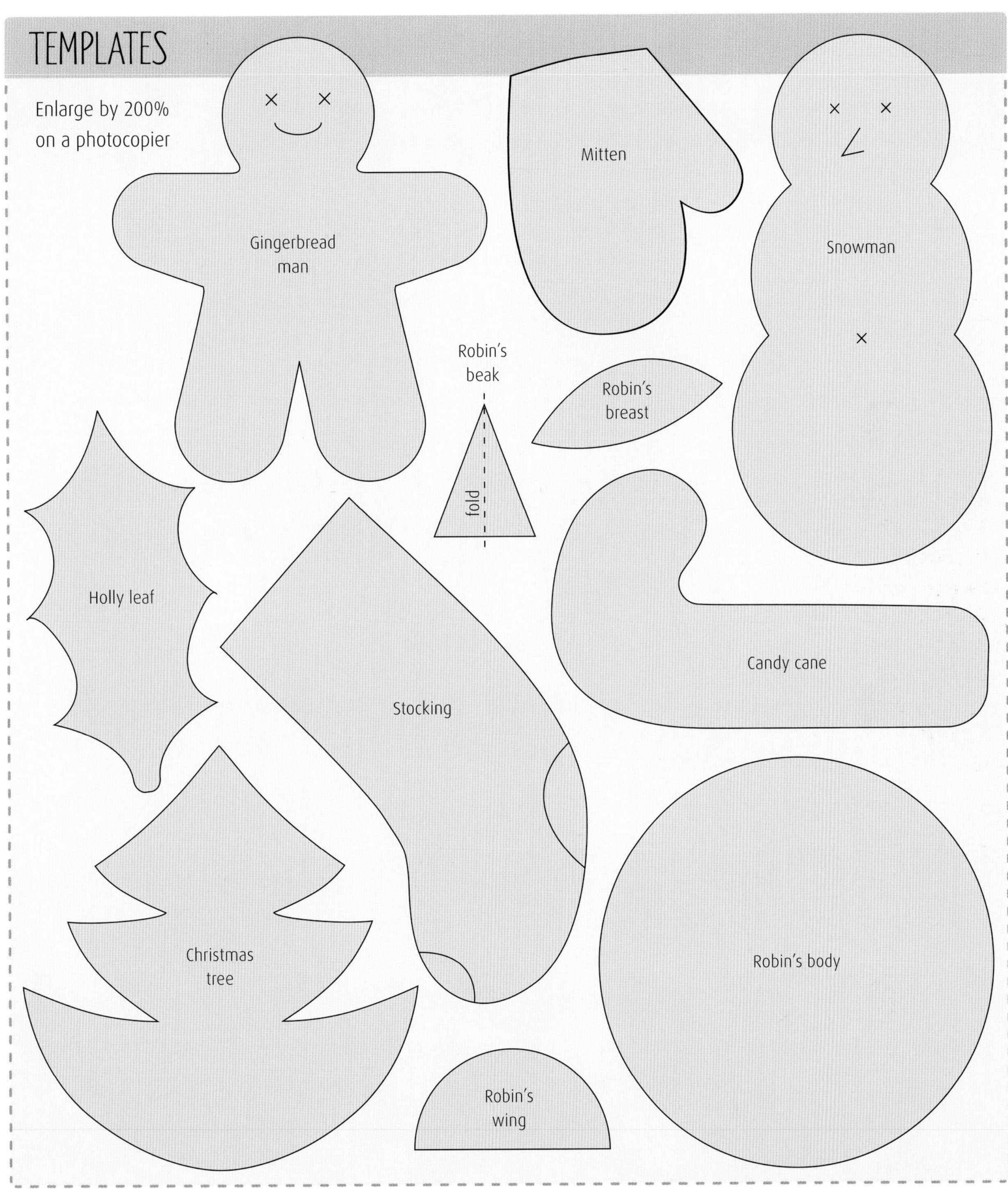

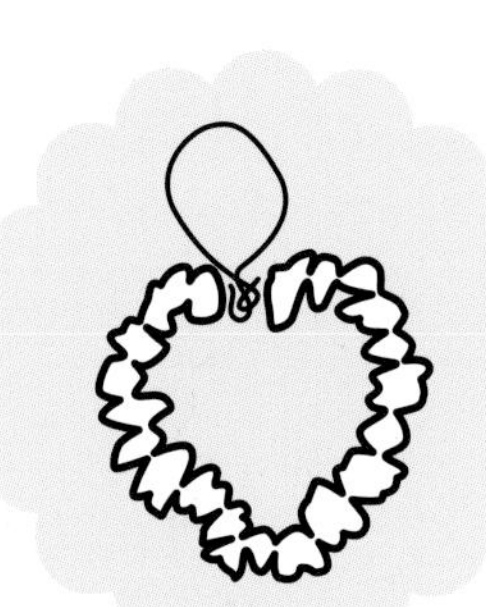

CHRISTMAS DECORATIONS

Dried fruit and foraged materials can be turned into stunning decorations that look rustic and make your home smell wonderful.

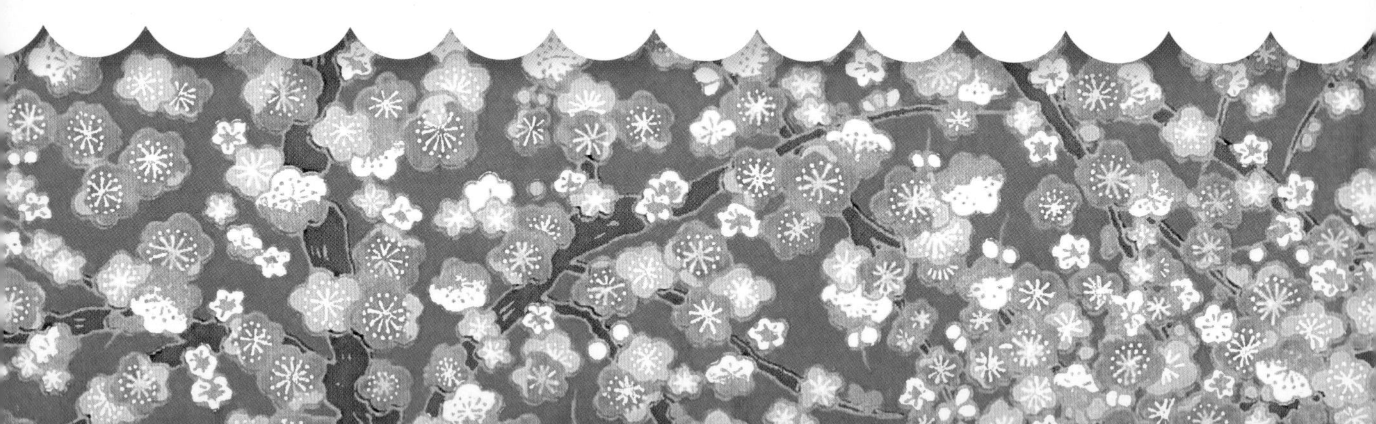

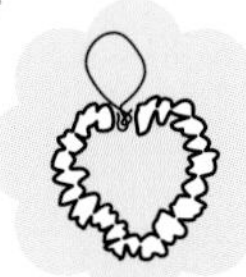

HOW TO MAKE DECORATIONS

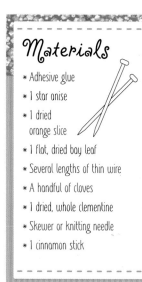

Materials

* Adhesive glue
* 1 star anise
* 1 dried orange slice
* 1 flat, dried bay leaf
* Several lengths of thin wire
* A handful of cloves
* 1 dried, whole clementine
* Skewer or knitting needle
* 1 cinnamon stick

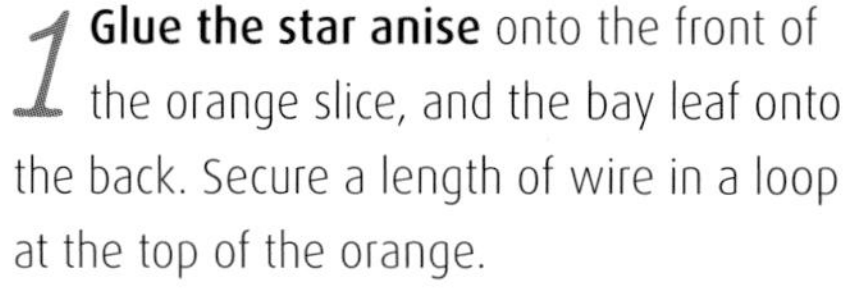

1 **Glue the star anise** onto the front of the orange slice, and the bay leaf onto the back. Secure a length of wire in a loop at the top of the orange.

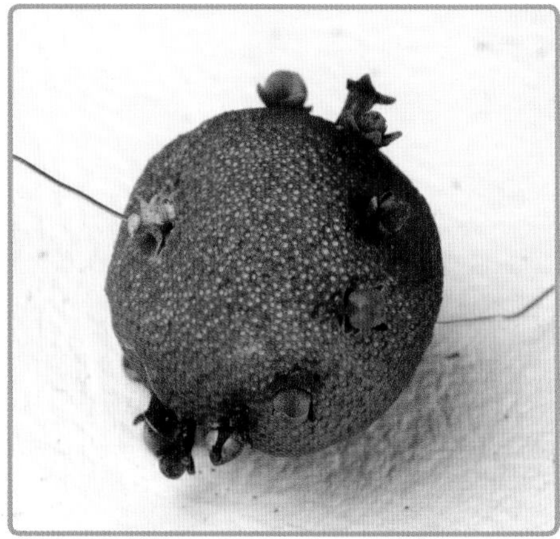

2 **Stick cloves into** the clementine in a pattern. Push a skewer through the fruit, thread wire through the hole and secure one end in a loop.

3 **Thread wire lengthways** through the cinnamon stick. Bend one end over, thread the other end through the clementine loop, and secure.

4 **Attach the loose** wire at the top of the clementine to the orange slice. The three parts should now all be joined together by wire.

VARIATIONS

Simple orange pomanders Make natural baubles by evenly scoring orange skins and slowly dehydrating the fruits.

Fruit and flower sprigs For simple, stylish decorations, tie stems of rosehips to dried teazle heads with wire and finish with a loop.

Citrus slices Make a hole in the top of a dried orange slice, thread through a length of string, and secure in a knot.

Cinnamon walnut bundles Attach a walnut at either end of a thin rope, wrap the rope around the sticks, and glue on a star anise.

Cranberry hearts Thread thin string through dried cranberries using a needle, secure in a heart shape, and finish with a loop.

Snow clouds Tie extra quantities of wispy or fluffy seed heads to Chinese lanterns with thin wire and finish with a loop.

WINTER WREATH

Wreaths are a great introduction to floristry, giving you a chance to work with both fresh and dried foliage. You could also add leaves, dried fruits, and nuts to create a design that is unique and smells gorgeous.

HOW TO MAKE A WINTER WREATH

Materials

* Stripped vine stems
* Scissors or secateurs
* Fine wire
* Selection of fresh foliage (fir sprigs, myrtle, berries, eucalyptus leaves)
* Measuring tape
* Selection of dried foliage (pine cones, acorns)
* Superglue
* Hook or ribbon
* Fragrance oil (optional)
* Spray bottle

1 **Follow making** a wreath frame (opposite) to make a 30cm (12in) diameter circular frame. Around six rounds of vine will make a thick, sturdy frame.

2 **Make 15 to 20 fir bunches** by winding wire around the bottom of the stems. Attach each one to the frame with wire so that they face the same direction. Overlap one bunch with the next to cover the frame.

3 **Trim the remaining** fresh foliage to size and arrange it around the wreath. Play with the design until you are happy with it before securing the foliage in place. Use a measuring tape to check that the spacing between the foliage is even.

4 **Tuck individual sprigs** of fresh foliage into the frame between the fir bunches. Attach other bunches of foliage with short lengths of wire, tucking the ends of the wire into the fir to hide them.

5 **Arrange the dried** foliage on top of the wreath to get an idea of the finished look, then glue in position.

6 **Hang the wreath** on a hook, or if you prefer, attach a ribbon at the top to hang it. You can scent it with a few drops of fragrance oil or leave it as it is. Spritz regularly with water to keep it fresh.

TECHNIQUES

Making a wreath frame

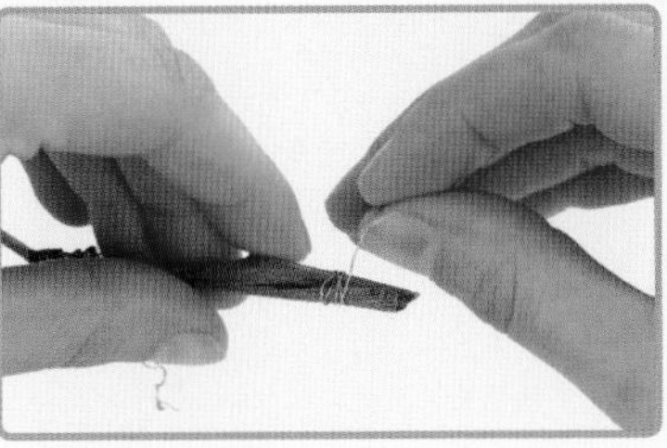

1 **Strip two equal** lengths of vine of their leaves. Secure them together by binding with a short length of fine wire.

2 **Twist the vines** together to make one strong length. Secure the other end with wire.

3 **Bring the two ends** together to create a circle. Twist the ends around each other and tie them together with a short length of wire. If the vines are too long, overlap the ends; if they're too short, introduce an additional length.

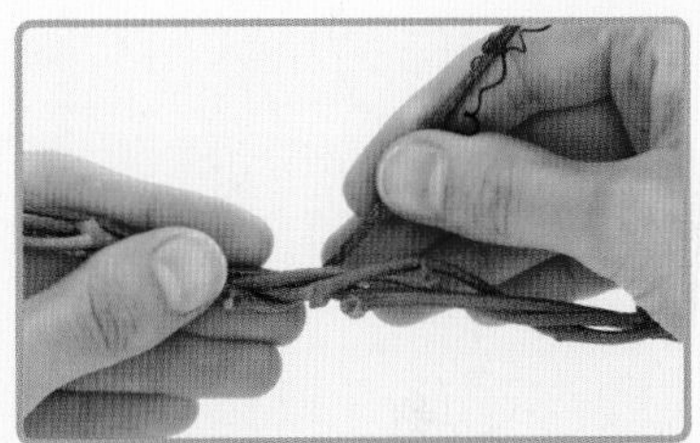

4 **To strengthen** the frame, add more lengths of stripped vine. Tie one end to the frame with wire and wind the vine around the frame, securing the other end with wire. Repeat until you have a strong, firm frame.

5 **To keep the shape** even and strengthen the frame more, tie small pieces of wire at regular intervals around the frame.

KNITTED HEARTS

A trio of hanging hearts that sport knitted and embroidered motifs. Perfect for Valentine's Day or just to give to a loved one.

HOW TO MAKE KNITTED HEARTS

Materials

* Debbie Bliss Rialto DK 50g
  A: 12 Scarlet x 1
  B: 01 White x 1
  C: 42 Pink x 1

A x 1 **B** x 1 **C** x 1

* 1 pair of 3.75mm (UK9/US5) needles
* Large-eyed needle
* Polyester toy stuffing
* 90cm (35in) x 6mm (1/4in) -wide red ribbon
* Sewing needle & red sewing thread
* 3 x 1cm (1/2in) mother-of-pearl buttons

TENSION
26sts and 30 rows to 10cm (4in) over st st on 3.75mm (UK9/US5) needles

WHITE HEART (MAKE 2)

(SEE P.215 FOR PICTURE)

Pattern

Using yarn B, cast on 3sts.
K 1 row and p 1 row.
Now shape sides as follows:
Row 1: K1, yon, k1, yon, k1.
Row 2: P1, yrn, p into back of yon on previous row, p1, p into back of yon on previous row, yrn, p1.
Row 3: K1, yon, k into back of yrn on previous row, k3, k into back of yrn on previous row, yon, k1.
Row 4: P1, yrn, p into back of yon on previous row, p5, p into back of yon on previous row, yrn, p1.
Row 5: K1, yon, k into back of yrn on previous row, k to last 2sts, k into back of yrn on previous row, yon, k1.
Row 6: P1, yrn, p into back of yon on previous row, p to last 2sts, p into back of yon on previous row, yrn, p1.
Rep the last 2 rows until there are 35sts, ending with a p row. *.
Following the chart, below right, work 14 rows in Fair Isle patt.
When chart is complete, work a further 6 rows st st using yarn B only.
Complete as given from All Hearts to end.

PINK HEART (MAKE 2)

Pattern

Using yarn C, work as for White Heart until there are 31sts, ending with a p row. Cont to shape sides as set until there are 35sts, at the same time now work in patt from Chart 2, opposite centre. Odd numbers are RS rows and read from right to left, even numbered rows are WS rows and read from left to right.
Use a separate ball of yarn for each area of colour, twisting yarns tog when joining colours to avoid a hole from forming. When chart is complete, work a further 6 rows st st using yarn C only.
Complete as given from All Hearts to end.

RED HEART (MAKE 2)

Pattern

Using yarn A, work as for White Heart to *

Cont in st st, beg with a k row, work 20 rows straight.

Complete as given from All Hearts to end.

ALL HEARTS

**Shape top

Next row: K17, turn and cont on these sts only for first side.

Now dec 1st at both ends of next 5 rows. (7sts)

Cast off.

With RS of work facing, rejoin yarn to rem sts. K2tog and then k to end.

Dec 1st at both ends of next 5 rows. (7sts)

Cast off.

Following the chart, below, and using yarn B, cross-stitch a heart in the centre of both sides.

Making up

Place front and back together with RS facing and stitch around outer edges, leaving a small opening in one straight edge. Turn RS out. Stuff the hearts and stitch closed. Cut a length of ribbon 30cm (12in) long and sew it to the top of the front with matching thread. Sew on one button to cover the raw ends of the ribbon.

CHARTS

KEY

Scarlet | White | Pink

White heart

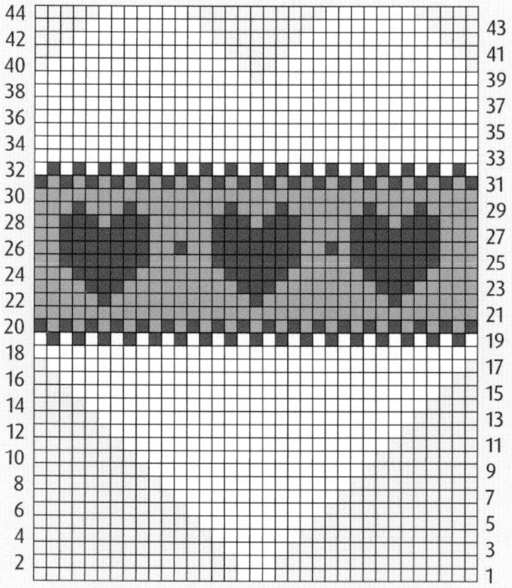

Pink heart

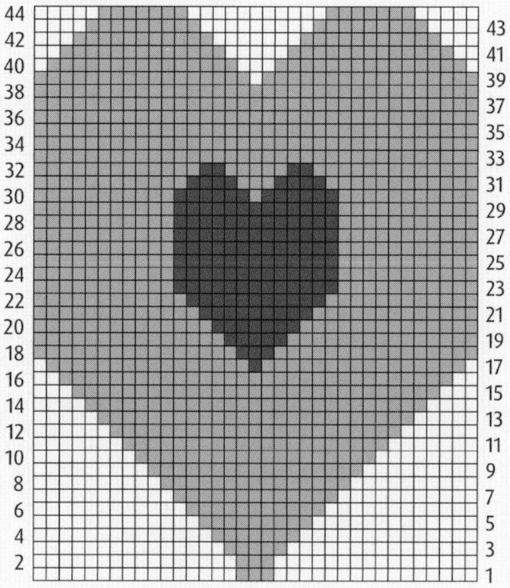

Red heart

CHOCOLATE TRUFFLES

These chocolate truffles look so impressive that you'll be surprised to find how easy they are to make. Coat them with cocoa and icing sugar for a classic look, or with various colourful toppings for a truly tempting box of treats.

HOW TO MAKE CHOCOLATE TRUFFLES

Makes 30 truffles

Ingredients

* 125ml (4fl oz) double cream
* 2 tbsp dark rum, brandy, or sherry
* 250g (9oz) plain, white, or milk chocolate, melted
* 40g (1½oz) cocoa
* 20g (¾oz) icing sugar

Equipment

* Saucepan
* Bowl
* Whisk
* Teaspoon
* Tray
* Greaseproof paper
* Sieve
* Plate

1 **Place the cream** in a saucepan, bring it to the boil to sterilize, then cool until lukewarm. Stir in the rum, brandy, or sherry, then add it to the cool, melted chocolate, stirring until blended.

2 **Beat the mixture** until light and fluffy, then chill for two-three hours until it is firm enough to divide into portions.

3 **Using a teaspoon**, scoop out balls of the mixture and roll into neat balls. Place them onto a tray lined with greaseproof paper, keeping them well apart. Chill until firm, about one hour.

4 **Sift the cocoa** and icing sugar together to create a sugar and cocoa coating.

5 **One at a time**, roll the chilled truffles in your hands to soften the outside slightly, then roll them in the cocoa and icing sugar mixture to coat.

TRY THESE TOPPINGS

To create a colourful array of truffles, divide the rolled balls into batches after they have been chilled. Roll each truffle in your hands quickly to soften the outside, then roll in your favourite toppings or try a more daring combination. Place the truffles in a gift box, cellophane wrap with pretty ribbons, or add cake-pop sticks to the bottom and use for a child's birthday party.

* Chopped pistachio nuts
* Chocolate vermicelli
* Dried strawberries
* Chopped hazelnuts
* Chopped pistachio nuts
* Desicated coconut
* Piped white chocolate
* Dark chocolate, chilli and cinnamon (mix just a pinch of cinnamon and cayenne pepper into melted dark chocolate)
* Dried raspberries and sea salt (use 1 tsp of sea salt flakes to every tablespoon of dried raspberries)

INDEX

ACKNOWLEDGMENTS

Dorling Kindersley would like to thank contributors who worked on the original books: Authors Sheherazade Goldsmith, Dr Vikki Haffenden, Claire Montgomerie, Philippa Pearson, Susannah Steele, Jennifer Wendell Kosek; Editors May Corfield, Katherine Goddard, Holly Kyte, Alastair Laing, Hilary Mandleberg, Corinne Masciocchi, Kathryn Meeker, James Mitchem, Laura Nickoll, Scarlett O'Hara, Laura Palosuo; Designers Charis Bhagianathan, Jane Ewart, Glenda Fisher, Gemma Glover, Sonia Moore, Vicky Read, Sara Robin, John Round, Ivy Roy, Caroline de Souza, Kathryn Wilding; Photographers Peter Anderson, Clive Bozzard-Hill, Ruth Jenkinson, William Revell; Crafters Barbara Coup, Lucy Harrington, Charlotte Johnson, Made in Hastings, Claire Montgomerie, The Oxford Soap Company, Francine Raymond, Clare Smith, Sparrowkids, Ted & Harry; Angela Baynham for proofreading; and Vanessa Bird for the index.